Dearest Andrew
For all your Saturdays
With love on your birthday   Imogen.
xx
Feb '05.

The Borough Market Book

From Roots to Renaissance

D1581813

With contributions from Ptolemy Dean, Sheila Dillon, Henrietta Green, Dominic Murphy, Jo French and Rachel de Thample.

Photography by Jason Lowe

CIVIC
books

THE BOROUGH MARKET BOOK

FROM ROOTS TO RENAISSANCE

The Borough Market Book:
From Roots to Renaissance
1st Edition Published by
Civic Books 2005.

Civic Books
6 Southwark Street
London SE1 1TQ, UK

Tel: +44 (0)20 7378 0422
Email: info@civicbooks.com
Web: www.civicbooks.com

ISBN: 1-904104-90-8
Copyright © Civic Books 2005
Photography Copyright ©
Jason Lowe.

British Library Cataloguing
in Publication Data.
A catalogue record for this
book is available from
the British Library.

Project developed by
Tobias Steed,
Can of Worms Publishing
in association with:
Editorial Director,
Miranda Glover
Art and Design Director,
Lawrence Morton
Production Director,
Geoff Barlow.

All Market Thoughts, Tips
and In My Basket interviews
were conducted by Rachel de
Thample.

The essay on Wholesale
Produce was derived from
articles in the Borough
Market News written by
Eleanor Wallis and others.

Printed and bound in Italy.

Thanks

This book would not be
possible without the
endorsement and support of
the Trustees of the Borough
Market and for the use of
the following images from
the Borough Market archive:
Pages 18 (left) and 20.
Copyright Trustees of the
Borough Market.

The London Metropolitan
Archives for their assistance
and support and providing
the following images:
Pages 17, 18 (top right), 19,
28, 162, and 163 (left).
Copyright the Corporation
of London, London
Metropolitan Archive.

Southwark Local Studies
Library for their assistance
and support and providing
the following images:
Pages 14, 160 and 161.

For the image on:
Page 16. Copyright V&A
Images/Victoria and Albert
Museum.

For the image on: Page 163
(right). Copyright
Charterhouse-in-Southwark.

The Chocolate Tart recipe on
page 136 is reproduced
courtesy of Sara-Jane
Staynes' book, *Chocolate:
The Definitive Guide*, by
Grub Street Publishing.

Our appreciation is extended
to many but in particular to
the architectural firm of
Greig + Stephenson Architects
(GSA), Southwark, London, for
their market expertise,
support and generosity.

Metro Imaging, Clerkenwell,
London.

DL Repro, Clerkenwell,
London

Roast for the creation of the
recipes.

Finally, we would like to
thank all market traders,
shoppers and staff of the
market who have given their
time for interviews,
thoughts and tips.

Recipes from Roast Throughout the Retail Produce section of this book recipes have been created that celebrate freshness, variety and something a little unusual or unexpected sourced from Borough Market. The food is lively, colourful and possible to prepare in 30 to 45 minutes, or less. None of the recipes require any special preparation that cannot be readily recreated in a domestic kitchen and all use core ingredients sourced from specific Borough Market stalls. The recipes also reflect seasonal variations and the regional stretch from which produce at Borough comes.

All the recipes have been created under the direction of restaurateur Iqbal Wahhab and chef de cuisine Henrietta Green, both of the new restaurant, *Roast*, which is taking up residence in the Floral Hall at Borough Market. The menu at *Roast* will constantly evolve, in order to make the most of market opportunities and seasonal trends. The restaurant is dedicated to celebrating the very best of British cooking, using the country's finest produce, and drawing from both ancient and modern dishes, as well as innovative cooking techniques.

Pan-fried Sirloin Steak with Wild Mushrooms 64

Pan-fried Pork Loin Chops with Cider Mustard Sauce 69

Poached Chicken Breast with Summer Vegetables 72

Marinated Smoked Haddock 79

Hake with Peas and Parsley 85

Potted Shrimps 88

Salad of Wood Pigeon, Wild Boar Pancetta and Mixed Leaves 95

Roasted Autumn Vegetables 104

Summer Fruit Soup with Thick Cream 108

Gypsy Toast with Roasted Plums and Clotted Cream 116

Brown Bread and Honey Ice Cream 126

Chocolate Tart 136

CONTENTS

Foreword 10
   by George Nicholson, Chairman of the Board of
   Trustees of Borough Market

London's Larder 12
   Roots to Revival by Ptolemy Dean 14
   Floral Portico by Jo French 24

The living market 30
   A Day in the Life 32
   Wholesale Produce 40
   Source to Stall by Dominic Murphy 46

   Retail Produce by Henrietta Green 54
      Meat, Game & Poultry 60
      Fish & Shellfish 76
      Deli & Store 90
      Fruit 'n Veg 98
      Bakery 112
      Dairy 120
      Treats & Snacks 130
      Drink 140

The bigger picture 148
   Thought for Food by Sheila Dillon 150
   Southwark Surrounds by Jo French 158

Market Traders' Directory 169

Ptolemy Dean *Architect, TV Presenter and Trustee of Borough Market* • Ptolemy is a presenter on the BBC's *Restoration* programme. He specialises in the repair of historic buildings and the design of new buildings on sensitive sites. He was responsible for the Millennium Project at Southwark Cathedral which has won eight awards, including those from the RIBA and Civic Trust. He currently enjoys a mix of projects including repairs and alterations to Malmesbury Abbey, St James's Piccadilly, and the Parish Churches of Devizes and Farnham. On the secular side, he is working on a number of country houses across England.

Sheila Dillon *Author and Radio Broadcaster* • Sheila presents BBC Radio 4's *The Food Programme*. She's been reporting on the politics of food since 1982. Her interest was triggered when a pesticide alert in New York, where she was living with her husband and baby at the time, made her realise that she had no idea what was going into her food. Now she knows.

Henrietta Green *Author and Gourmand* • Henrietta is acknowledged as the country's leading expert on Britain's speciality food producers. Passionate to support and develop them, she runs countrywide *Food Lovers' Fairs,* www.foodloversbritain.com. She is also Director of Cuisine at the new restaurant, *Roast,* in the Floral Hall at Borough Market. A showcase for Britain's finest, seasonal produce, *Roast* will champion small, regional producers.

Dominic Murphy *Journalist* • Dominic writes for *The Guardian,* where his duties include the *Green Consumer* column in *Weekend* magazine. It follows that fresh, unadulterated food is close to his heart — this was the main reason for his recent move to a house in Dorset with a large garden, where he is planning to grow his own vegetables.

Jo French *Author, Archivist* • Jo studied with the Open University, then completed an MA in London studies at Birkbeck, specialising in the historical geography of the city. Jo is a freelance researcher, writer and architectural librarian, and works part-time with Greig + Stephenson Architects. She is also co-editor of *Tooley's Dictionary of Mapmakers*.

Rachel de Thample *Journalist* • Rachel first discovered Borough Market when she was editing an online property magazine in Southwark. Visiting the market brought out her passion for food, so she became a restaurant PR consultant, worked as a chef in Marco Pierre White's *Quo Vadis* in Soho, and is currently commissioning editor of *Waitrose Food Illustrated*.

Jason Lowe *Photographer* • Jason Lowe and his daughter are often found in Borough on a Saturday morning. He photographs food for, amongst others, *The Independent Saturday magazine* with Mark Hix, *Saveur* and *Gourmet Traveller* in the States. Jason has photographed a long list of recipe books including the new *St John* restaurant *Nose to Tail Eating* and the new Henry Harris, *A Passion for Protein;* and has picked up two Glenfiddich awards for the trouble.

FOREWORD

Borough Market – a celebration! This book is intended as a milestone and a signpost. The former – a cause for some celebration, is the physical renewal of this ancient market. The latter – an expression of hope – that Borough Market is on the way to becoming one of the best markets in Europe. More modestly perhaps, I hope too that the book provides a pointer to other markets looking for fresh inspiration, and also for future residents who will take over the baton as trustees in years to come.

Back from the brink We have come a long way since when at a meeting of trustees almost ten years ago, presided over by the then chairman; Ted Bowman, we faced the prospect of financial melt-down. Years of decline in the wholesale trade – a product of changing consumer shopping patterns – had meant that, not only was there a lot of vacant space in the market, but insufficient funds were available to maintain its increasingly decrepit structures and services. New health regulations for wholesale markets completed the challenge facing the then board of trustees. Given the recent past, it was not immediately obvious that the solution might lie in the core business of the market itself: the selling of food.

But it was the memory of the existence of a retail element within Borough Market in an earlier century that contained the seed of an idea that was to become our eventual saviour. An architectural competition in 1995, won by Greig + Stephenson, kick started the process of renewal. Long standing wholesalers such as Andrew Sugarman, Chairman of the Regeneration Board and the Market Tenants' Association, gave up countless hours with other traders and trustees as the project progressed, in addition to working through the night. Threading a path through changes in government and different funding bodies has required a magician's skills. But it has not all been a slog, indeed it has been a fascinating journey of discovery, starting as London's "best kept secret" and culminating with Borough Market being voted "The best market in Britain" by the *Observer Food Monthly* magazine. We have now arrived at a position where the risk taken and the faith put in us by organisations like the London Development Agency have been rewarded.

What is Borough Market? Most people know it today as a bustling retail food market. But, for much of the last century at least, it was best known as a wholesale fruit and vegetable market. Today, despite its relative decline, the wholesale business still lies at the core of the operation, and in the trustees' eyes, provides its soul. A series of statutes stretching back to the mid-eighteenth century spell out the nature and functions of the market and the duties of its trustees. More recently, it was the acknowledgment of the long standing "social purpose" of holding a market that led to it being registered as a charity. The market has, of course, evolved over the centuries, as described elsewhere, but its very essence – "a concourse of buyers and sellers" – remains the same. However, there never has been just one strand to Borough Market's bow. As well as the wholesale and retail market; shops, warehouses, cellars, stands and stalls, have all contributed to the rich entity that is "The Market".

A happy accident? Recent years have seen the growth of farmers' markets and a more general interest in food in this country. It is long overdue. Borough Market is part of this process, indeed, we like to think we are now at the forefront of those seeking to develop a new attitude to food, its production and distribution. But none of what we have achieved and are now seeking to promote would have been possible if it weren't for the arrival in 1986 of Randolph Hodgson and his Neil's Yard Dairy, or, subsequently, in 1998 of Henrietta Green's *Food Lovers' Fair*. From those early pioneering days with at best half a dozen stalls, the market has grown into an amazing cornucopia, over a hundred strong. This hasn't all been a happy accident. An alliance forged early on between trustees and traders has been the key to our success. James Todd, the vice chairman, and I might have had the enthusiasm and the odd dash of vision, but it was the experience willingly shared by early traders such as Peter Gott, a wild boar farmer from Cumbria, and those he encouraged to come and chance their arm, that created the momentum behind the new retail market. Borough Market has never attempted or claimed to be a farmers' market. A mixture of geography, history and curiosity meant that we took to developing a wider canvas, more akin to markets elsewhere in Europe, but almost unknown in the UK. Alongside fresh farm produce from Lincolnshire you will find stalls selling the best olive oils from Italy, cheeses from France, tomatoes from the Isle of Wight, teas from the East, pies from Leicestershire, hams from Spain and Highland beef from Preston. Trader selection has been steered throughout by Chris Denning, the market manager, and a food committee comprising trustees and traders, who very early on decided that promoting quality produce would be the hallmark of Borough Market. It is a decision that has served us well and is one that other markets will undoubtedly need to follow if they are to survive in the competitive environment in which we now operate.

The future Where do we go from here? This book, based on our experience, is intended as a point of reference for those who might be thinking of embarking on a similar route to that we took ten years ago. I have no doubt over time that markets similar to the one at Borough will evolve in other cities around the UK. Indeed, for the number of producers to grow in this country, that evolution is essential. There already is a growing network of organisations promoting regional produce. But for markets to thrive in the long term, both the authorities that own them and the traders that occupy them need to embark on a radical re-think of what it is they are offering and why. The focus of this re-think needs to be the consumer on the one hand and the producer on the other. Competing on price with superstores is a dead end – literally. Competing on quality, value and choice, in the knowledge that this could start to underpin a fundamentally different attitude to food and the way we produce it, buy it and eat it, is a rich seam that we have only just started to explore. Join us!

George Nicholson *Chairman of the Board of Trustees of Borough Market.*

London's Larder

19th century horse drawn bus at east end of Southwark Cathedral. The short lived domed roof of the market can be seen in the background.

ROOTS TO REVIVAL

BY PTOLEMY DEAN

The recent renaissance of Borough Market has helped turn what was a depressed inner-city suburb into a thriving community once more. Remarkably, at the core of its revival lie roots that stretch back hundreds of years, and whose influence can be felt in the very fabric of its contemporary useage, and the redevelopment of its historic architecture.

Left: The Tabard Inn prior to
its demolition in 1875.
Right: The Borough Market
House, sketch dated 1810.

Go to any European city and at the heart of it you will find a dedicated food market of one sort or another. This invariably takes the form of a covered structure which bustles with traders and overspills into the streets nearby. These places throng with life and are much to be preferred to the lifeless supermarkets and wholesale distribution depots that no doubt achieve a higher 'health and hygiene' rating. Markets are a honey pot of activity and commerce – hardly surprising, given that cities only came about in the first place for gathering and trading. In London our city fathers have somehow found this life and the inevitable congestion that it causes rather too much to bear. Traditional city markets have become an endangered species, threatened with extinction. Covent Garden fruit and vegetable market and Billingsgate Fish Market were both banished to the suburbs in the 1970s; the first to a desolate concrete bunker near Vauxhall, the second to a dreary compound of tin sheds on the Isle of Dogs. The old buildings at Covent Garden were saved at the eleventh hour and have become a 'heritage attraction', while the old Billingsgate is now an office block, having narrowly escaped a road widening scheme. The stamping out of covered markets continues to this day. Most of Spitalfields Market was recently demolished for more offices, while much of Smithfield Meat Market is now threatened with a similar fate.

For a while Borough Market also looked doomed. Plans to drive a new railway line through its glass roofs on a crudely designed concrete viaduct still exist as part of the long delayed Thameslink 2000 scheme. This may yet happen, but the painstaking repair and regeneration of the central section of the market has been carried out regardless. Indeed rather than giving up the fight, the market has been positively defiant, adding to its historic buildings rather than sweeping them away. The resurrection of a part of the old Floral Hall is positively inspired. What was Covent Garden's loss has become the Borough's gain, and the newly placed portico somehow looks more at home in SE1 than it ever did in WC2. In this context, the survival of Borough Market, both as a wholesale fruit and vegetable market at night, and a popular retail produce market at weekends, is nothing short of a miracle. As the whole Borough area revives it is becoming once more the vital part of London that it was in medieval times, and we should rejoice in the contribution that the restored market is making. Dead streets round about have re-awoken, and people are flocking to live here. The place heaves with visitors and Londoners alike.

Borough Market is arguably London's most evocative and picturesque covered market. Although much of what can be seen above ground is largely Victorian or twentieth century in date, there is a sense of the 'medieval' that permeates its site, and colours its atmosphere accordingly. There are no great vistas here and none of the great rectangular architectural set pieces of the Spitalfields, Smithfield,

SECTION BB

WROT IRON COVER PLATE OVER SIDE COLUMNS (N⁰ 6 OF THESE)

N⁰ 11 Of these brackets required.

Also One cast shew

Also One cast shew with bolt holes arranged to suit position

— DETAILS OF NEW BRACKETS —

W.A.CONFORD

Billingsgate or Covent Garden type. Instead there are sections of roof that are twisted and distorted to fit into whatever shape was available. Look up and a cast iron barrel vault might rise where it is least expected. A street edge will be celebrated with an ornamental timber awning supported on fancy iron brackets. A network of footpaths skirt around a forest of iron supporting columns and squeeze themselves through the numerous sooty brick arches of the Victorian railway viaducts that criss-cross overhead. It is frankly a bit of a muddle, but the cutting through of new streets and elevated railways have left this ancient and awkwardly shaped site in tact. Indeed so complex are the geometries of its make up that it would now be difficult to redevelop, and it is perhaps this, more than anything else, that has saved the market from some other use.

Markets in the Borough area have had as long a history as London itself. The Borough High Street connected the southern end of London Bridge, the sole crossing point of the Thames, with the pilgrims' routes to the south west (Winchester) and the south east (Canterbury and Dover), approximately today's A3 and A2. Being outside of the jurisdiction of the City of London, this area soon became congested with inns, taverns, and the sorts of dispossessed persons that the City wished to keep out. Prisons and brothels have always been a feature of the area. A market vested by Edward VI occupied the wide section of Borough High

Street just south of the present Old Town Hall Chambers. Up to the Reformation this was the site of the old parish church of St Margaret's. Even today, the swelling in the street width here recalls the sense of an ancient market place, despite the mess of modern day traffic, engineering and signage.

In 1691 the Court Leet of Southwark ordered that the "Market shall be kept on the west side of the channel of the High Street within this Borough beginning at the Bridge Foot". In other words they had it moved northwards to what must have already been a fairly congested point at the southern end of London Bridge. The traffic jams and muddle caused by the market must have backed up for miles, blocking the sole southern exits from the City. Not surprisingly, in 1755 the City of London Corporation successfully petitioned for its abolition. But this would not be the end of it. A successful petition to Parliament by the churchwardens and parishioners of St Saviour's, Southwark, created a replacement market a year later on the present site, then known as 'the triangle', which was far enough away from the main road to avoid congestion. St Saviour's, today's cathedral, was a substantial former priory that had been taken over by the parish to replace the cramped old St Margaret's on Borough High Street. The aims of the new market were, and remain, two-fold: to hold a market, and to contribute profit from the market for the relief of the poor. Today's market, in the shadow of St Saviour's, still

Opposite far left: Interior historic view of the market, showing its elaborate cast iron brackets.
Opposite above left: Architectural detail, drawing by Henry Jarvis, 1880.
Opposite below left: Historic photographic prints hanging in the market today.
Right: Drawing of the Bridge Approach with the Beare and Infant market.

contributes a financial relief to the Council Tax payers in the Parish of St Saviour's. Early impressions of the market are vague. The Rocque plan of 1761 shows the market area quite open with only modest sized blocks. One can imagine the character of the area from the street names. Modern Park Street was once known as 'Harrow Corner', 'Dead Man's Place' and 'Maid Lane', the latter presumably in celebration of what could be found along its length after hours. A sketch dated 1810 shows a rather countrified timber framed Borough Market building with a delicate cupola. Three years later, in 1813, cast iron bollards were installed, a somewhat delayed response to an Act of 1786 for 'paving, cleaning, lighting and watching the Streets, Lanes and other Publick [sic] Passages within the Manor of Southwark otherwise called The Clink'. Some of these bollards survive today. They are amongst the earliest purpose designed bollards in London.

The greatest changes to the Market and to Southwark as a whole came in the nineteenth century. These were caused by a revolution in transportation and movement within the city. In 1831, old medieval London Bridge was rebuilt 180 feet to the west of the original, clipping the eastern extremity of Southwark Cathedral and resulting in the reconstruction of the buildings along the eastern edge of the market. London Bridge railway station came in 1843, London's first railway terminus. Southwark Street was cut through to provide easier road access to it from the West End in the 1860s. But this would not be enough for the South Eastern Railway Company who wanted to take their trains beyond London Bridge directly in to the City and West End. This new line would be ruinously expensive to construct, involving two new railway bridges across the Thames, two new railway hotels at the Cannon Street and Charing Cross terminals, a replacement St Thomas's Hospital on a new site opposite the Palace of Westminster and new covered structures at Borough Market. The Borough Market was all but buried under the triangular railway junction between the Cannon Street and Charing Cross railway lines. These viaducts narrowly missed a substantial 88 foot high cast iron dome which had been erected over 'the triangle' in 1859 by Edward Habershon. It can be glimpsed rising above the new railway tracks in an early photographic view of a horse drawn bus posing by the eastern end of Southwark Cathedral, while the circular plan of columns imprinted can be seen on the 1873 edition OS map. Other structures were rebuilt as a direct result of the construction of the railway, and include the large covered structure just north of the Cannon Street branch on Cathedral Street. Given its close likeness to a railway station is hardly surprising given its origins.

The great Borough Market dome had a short life. A tall structure, no doubt hurriedly built and supported by flimsy iron columns repeatedly shaken by new railways on all sides, had little chance of survival. Elaborate proposals for its

Left: Cast Iron bollards first installed in 1813.

20

reconstruction by Henry Jarvis in 1880 survive in the London Metropolitan Archive, but it appears that the current much simpler and lower barrel-vaulted replacement structure was built instead. Another proposal, this time for the site south of the Charing Cross line at Stoney Street by Kinniple & Jaffrey from 1894, shows another most elaborate scheme. Again the present, but simpler, pair of barrel-vaulted roofs were built in its place. These vaults retain some of the most attractive and swirly decorated cast iron brackets of any structure on the market. They should be enjoyed for now as the proposed Thameslink 2000 line would cause the demolition of these vaults.

The twentieth century saw the market transformed again, this time as a result of its success and expansion as a wholesale market. 'During 1933 it is estimated that 1,750,000 bushels of vegetables... 300,000 bags of greens, 50,000 tons of sack vegetables – such as potatoes, turnips and parsnips – 250,000 boxes of fruit, 500,000 pecks of loose fruits, and 350,000 rolls of celery... were sold at the Borough Market', according to WJ Passingham in 'London Markets'. Expansion was inevitable, and the market spread south eastwards over the site of the ancient Three Crowns Square. Arthur W Cooksey and Partner's new building gave the market its first direct entrance from the Borough High Street since its relocation in 1756. In style it combined the 'art deco' and 'neo-Georgian' styles with the then fashionable 'hygienic' character of a hospital, all conveyed by shiny terrazzo floors and smooth veneered panelling. In a gesture of what could only be termed escapism, it was given a roof of jolly red pantiles as if transplanted from the South of France or the Californian coast. When completed it must have been in stark contrast to the grimy Dickensian character of the old market, at that time almost permanently engulfed in the smoke of passing steam trains. Cooksey's new building provided accommodation for the trustees meeting room and market offices, which were relocated from a fine arts and crafts styled building at No.1 Cathedral Street. At the same time, a new covered roadway was driven through the market to connect Borough High Street with the east end of Park Street. This was the last major work carried out at the market. Wartime bombing destroyed parts of the covered structure on Park Street, eventually replaced by a drab prefabricated concrete structure. The Borough volume of the 'Survey of London' written in 1950 summed up how undesirable the area had become: "The average sightseer in London is apt to avoid Southwark, thinking of it as a gloomy and crowded area of wharfs and factories". By the late 1960s, the riverside warehouses had been abandoned and had become vulnerable to arson. Although the wholesale market continued at night, the atmosphere by day was one of emptiness and general decline.

Thirty years on the transformation from this can hardly be believed. The riverside path has recreated a walking route along the Thames. At Borough Market, a bi-monthly retail market soon became weekly, and then twice weekly. For many, even among Londoners, the rediscovery of Southwark has come as quite a revelation. Phase I of the recent building works, completed by the architectural firm Greig + Stephenson, have transformed the market and added a new dimension. The new Floral Hall connects to a modern building which is forced to take a triangular plan. New lighting and a new livery of green and silver paint have transformed the Victorian roof structures into objects of wonder and beauty. It will be embarrassing for Network Rail to try and take any part of them down.

The vision of the trustees to commit to this work, and the generosity of a regeneration grant to partly fund it should be applauded. It is very much hoped that the work will continue to future phases.

FOR MANY,
EVEN AMONG LONDONERS,
THE REDISCOVERY OF SOUTHWARK
HAS COME AS
QUITE A REVELATION.

Market thoughts

George Nicholson
Chairman of the Board of Trustees of Borough Market.

I was born in Southwark – well in Camberwell as it then was and I've lived in "The Borough" for over 30 years. My links with the area go back a long way, both my grandparents having been head-teachers in elementary schools in Waterloo over a century ago. I became a trustee of the market in the early '70s. It's an honorary position. There is no salary involved. To become a trustee you're nominated through the local council. I have loved being involved with the community along with many other people who have actively taken part in pursuing local improvements.

The "supermarket revolution" of the '70s and '80s saw a real shift away from local greengrocers and street markets. That is when the wholesale market in Borough started to go into decline. By 1995 it was clear to the trustees that something had to happen for it to survive. To add to our problems, our statutes do not allow us to borrow money, so it was a very difficult and tortuous process to get the funding together to regenerate the market.

From the start we were determined not to replicate the model of Covent Garden following its change in status. We chose a different path, focusing on quality food rather than general merchandising. That has proved to be the right decision because, as well as now having a thriving market, the finances of the trust have also been restored.

I'm also involved in the Coin Street project, which has transformed the riverfront around the OXO Tower into a thriving mixed community. When we started in 1984 few people came across to the South Bank. Now with Gabriel's Wharf, the OXO Tower and other attractions along the riverside, the number of visitors coming there is phenomenal. Following school, I originally trained in Liverpool as a ship's engineer. I come from a sea-faring family. It's nice having left the boats to maintain a link with the waterfront through these projects.

Markets are very social places, as well as centres of trade. It's that social dimension that underpins the reason for our charity status. From the feedback we get it's clear the market does play an important part in a lot of people's lives. The growing link between the town and country is another important dimension.

Britain has a "cheap food" mentality stemming from the postwar rationing years and farming subsidies. The idea of what represents good value is also very confused. At Borough we are trying to help get across that quality food, whilst good value, is not necessarily cheap. I believe that for the food revolution in this country to grow, there must be other markets similar to Borough Market in other cities. I am sure that other cities such as Birmingham, Leeds or Bristol will eventually develop a similar model.

I am proud to have helped redevelop Borough Market. We've gone from being an embarrassment to Southwark to being a major attraction, and one that also helps develop the wider area.

FLORAL PORTICO

BY JO FRENCH

The Floral Hall Portico, formerly of Covent Garden Market, was bought for just £1 by the Trustees of Borough Market. Architects Greig+Stephenson have ingeniously integrated the structure into their redevelopment programme and it now takes pride of place as the centrepiece of the regeneration project, accommodating both stalls and a restaurant, too.

If visiting Borough Market for the first time, you might be forgiven for assuming that the Floral Hall Portico in Stoney Street is one of its original Victorian market buildings. Its scale and the style of its façade are so appropriate it's hard to appreciate that this delightful cast iron and glass structure is a recent refugee. It forms the centrepiece of a major redevelopment programme as well as the new entry point to a range of refurbished buildings in Borough's ancient market. And its history is a curious tale of two markets that, until now, have followed very different paths – one consolidating on its ancient trading role, the other turning its back on its market origins.

The venerable old Borough Market has flourished on the southern approach to London Bridge since at least the early eleventh century and possibly since Roman times. It has occupied its present site in the shadow of Southwark Cathedral since 1756, over the years adding a mixture of market buildings and experiencing a variety of changes in its fortunes. Throughout the twentieth century Borough served largely as a wholesale market but by the 1980s and 1990s a spiral of decline in trade could have forced the market function to be abandoned. The trustees of Borough Market, for centuries the market's champions in good times and bad, were undaunted and determined that the ancient role of the market should continue and flourish. They had the vision to engineer a revival of the lost retail element of the market by planning a quality food venue – 'London's Larder'. This retail market was to complement the surviving wholesale trade.

However, the infrastructure was crumbling, and for the project to succeed the trustees had to regenerate the area by enhancing the physical market heritage. The market still had some impressive iron market structures ripe for restoration, but many of the buildings, including the great dome, had been lost either to railway encroachment in the mid-nineteenth century or to subsequent fire. George Nicholson, trustee, and former chairman of the GLC planning committee, thought the abandoned portico from Covent Garden's Floral Hall would be the perfect addition – matching the surviving buildings in date and purpose.

This is where the second, and now defunct, market comes in. Covent Garden

Market was established in Inigo Jones' Piazza in 1670, and had taken firm hold of the site by the nineteenth century when plans were hatched to add a floral hall. Frederick Gye, then the manager of the Italian Opera at Covent Garden, had first commissioned Edward Middleton Barry to design a new theatre after the previous one had been destroyed by fire in 1856. Gye's vision was ambitious, and a new market hall for exotic plants and flowers was added to Barry's commission, later to take shape next to the new Opera House.

As originally built, the Floral Hall was an impressive and innovative building with a delicate and ornate cast iron and glass structure, a glass dome, round-headed windows and a semi-circular glass roof. The cast pieces, made by iron-founder Henry Grissell of the Regent's Canal Ironworks, are dated 1859. On completion in 1860, the Floral Hall was much admired architecturally and favourably reviewed in the *Architects Journal* at that time, but partly sabotaged by friction between Gye and the Bedford Estate, it was never a great commercial success. The flower traders were more interested in practicality than aesthetics and preferred the rival site to the

south owned by the Bedford Estate (now the London Transport Museum).

Instead the Floral Hall served as a tea party and ball space, and from 1878, after the death of Gye, as a foreign fruit market. Miraculously, the building survived the Blitz, only to lose its dome and roof when it was severely damaged by fire in 1956. No longer an impressive survivor, the future for the Floral Hall looked bleak. It was saved physically when fierce local opposition prevented the wholesale redevelopment of Covent Garden Piazza, but the departure of the wholesale market for Nine Elms left the diminished Floral Hall functionally high and dry. The majority of it was incorporated into the Opera House as the Vilar Floral Hall, but of more interest to us is the one small part left languishing in the Opera's storerooms in Wales – the portico which had originally faced onto the Piazza.

So back to Southwark. Famously, it cost the trustees of Borough Market a mere £1 to acquire the redundant pieces for Borough, but to incorporate them into a viable and useful market building was not an easy task. Greig + Stephenson, the project architects, tried numerous options in their search for a way of incorporating the

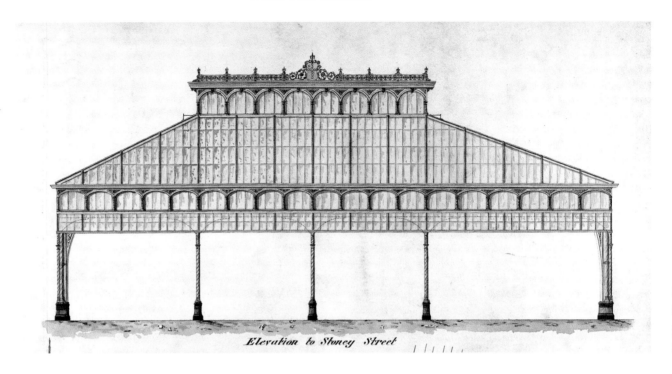

Elevation to Stoney Street

**Left: Elevation of
Stoney Street, a
proposal from Kinniple
& Jaffrey, 1894.**

portico into the market layout and infrastructure to best effect. The site eventually chosen on Stoney Street was an awkward triangular one, but had the most potential in terms of aesthetics, offering views of the portico from Stoney Street, Park Street and the railways. It would also allow the replacement of an unremarkable 1950s structure that had been built after the previous Victorian warehouse had been lost to fire in 1940. The portico would be just the front part of a modern building squeezed back between the old market and the railway viaduct. As the purpose was for the new structure to enhance the social and commercial functioning of the market as a whole, the worry was that open access to the trading action would be hampered by a building on this site. The solution was to follow the precedent set by the lost Victorian warehouse, leaving the ground floor of the building open to allow full permeability into the market.

While excavations and groundworks were underway, and the restoration of the other market buildings began, the cast pieces of the portico were brought out of storage to be cleaned and repaired ready for reconstruction. Inspired by the glorious fanlight and pitched roof that once covered the Stoney Street entrance to

Borough Market, new castings were made to replace the lost upper level of the portico façade. The new building which took shape also incorporated a row of abandoned columns and arches from the original Floral Hall at Covent Garden, and some spare new castings which were not used at the Royal Opera House. The rest of the building is uncompromisingly modern, with fully glazed sides looking over the bustle of the market to the east, and over the railway viaducts to St Paul's Cathedral and the City on the other side. Deep in the heart of the market, at the apex of the triangular site, a bull nose in knapped flint refers to the material used to face Southwark Cathedral.

The resulting Floral Hall Portico building faces a more certain future than the Floral Hall ever did at Covent Garden. Not only does it already have traders at ground floor level, it also again serves a leisure function as a restaurant on the first floor. Many years after its original construction, the Floral Hall Portico is finally serving the purpose for which Gye always intended it – as part of a thriving market. Now, within the scale and context of Borough Market and the nearby railways, it is as impressive and appropriate as if it had always been there.

Market thoughts

Ken Greig
Partner and co-founder Greig + Stephenson Architects (GSA).

We won a competition in 1995. The brief asked us to create a design for the retail market, but it didn't say what kind of market, so it could have been anything from clothes to antiques. The great danger of food markets is that what they sell has a shelf life. Food doesn't tend to afford the level of rents that leather jackets and jeans do. That's why most markets become a poor man's fashion parade.

The area between London Bridge and Tower Bridge was known as the 'pool' of London. This is where nearly all the food for London used to come into in the eighteenth and nineteenth centuries. It's been nicknamed 'London's Larder'. Borough Market is a strange and subterranean world. It lives beneath the viaducts and trains. It's like a basement.

Markets need a historical landmark. This gives them an immediate backdrop and identity. So to have Southwark Cathedral as a backdrop to Borough Market is quite extraordinary.

I grew up in the '50s and '60s. During this time, whole towns were ripped to pieces by motorways. It's taken 30 to 40 years for those areas to be repaired.

London's architecturally chaotic. The area of Borough is not like Bath, where you have a monolithic series of terraces. Instead, you have individual buildings, jostled together, fighting for space. That's the beauty of London.

Colour is a material. If you use colour inappropriately, you get the wrong kind of image. The topic of colour became hugely controversial when we painted the Floral Hall silver. People wanted it to be green.

Markets are all about the noise and the smells. You get totally taken in. Sometimes it's a bit chaotic, like a circus, but that's why it's full of people every weekend. They want to be part of the madness.

Southwark used to be the place where rules could be broken. Historically, the people working in the City of London would cross the river in the evening to pick up prostitutes and to gamble. It was the 'leisure centre' of London.

You only really get started as an architect when you're in your 50s. Until then, you have to serve your time. You can't be too much of a megalomaniac. I think it's wrong for architects to make building concrete – so it can never change.

Food is part of our lives. Sometimes all I can think about is my next meal. I could be in Italy, for instance, looking at the most amazing pieces of art, but I'll be standing there thinking about what I'm going to have for lunch or dinner. The architecture and design doesn't matter at the end of the day, it's what you can buy at the market that's important.

The living market

A DAY IN THE LIFE

For centuries the Borough Market has been supplying food to London and surrounding counties. Chances are that even if you have never had the pleasure of shopping in the retail market that you may have bought produce sourced by local greengrocers and restaurateurs from the wholesale market. This is a day in the life of 'London's Larder'.

While most of us are asleep the soul of Borough Market, its wholesale trade, is up and running and catering to a diverse clientele. Across the country trucks and transit vans are heading for Borough, following routes travelled for centuries.

10pm

From 10pm onwards lorries laden with produce recently plucked from the fields of Britain and the continent arrive at Borough Market.

They are unloaded in Stoney Street by a team of 'pitching porters' piling mounds of produce on the traders stands to await the arrival of customers.

12pm

The Trustees own 'police force', the Beadles, who until the 1930s used to have powers of arrest and the use of cells under the market (recently re-discovered), maintain good order throughout. In operation since the 17th century, they were traditionally employed to protect a parliamentary statute stipulating that no one could offer goods for sale within 1000 yards of Borough Market, unless

2am

4am

tolls or rents had been paid. Whilst produce is still being unloaded, the salesmen and cashiers arrive to get their wholesale cages in order and to prepare themselves for the next few hours of hard trading.

In the early hours, greengrocers, restaurateurs and hoteliers from the City, West End and the South East come to select the freshest produce available. They are a familiar crowd who do regular business at the market and there is a happy banter between traders and buyers as deals are done.

The greengrocers tend to be the fussier buyers, as they know the produce has to look good in their shops. The caterers are more interested in what tastes good, so they can look for the better bargains. This is when the bidding begins, as no price is set in stone.

From the smallest corner shops to large retailers, each and every transaction is negotiated, the prices determined by both quantity and quality. The final price will be dependent on how long the produce has been with the wholesaler, and on the quantity bought. It might be anything from one to 100 boxes of any given item.

When a deal has been struck, the sold boxes are put on pallets and loaded on to the customer's van by fork-lift truck to be taken on to their next destination.

6am

On Friday mornings Phillip Dampier begins setting up the retail market for the trustees at around 6am. First of all he puts up the umbrella stands for the uncovered Green Market, then he empties all the bins and removes any pallets lying around. On Saturdays, when the retail market opens earlier, he has to start the whole process two hours earlier, at 4am.

By now Maria of Maria's Market Café has her griddle hot, her kettles boiling and tea brewing. The wholesalers cap off their 'day' with a cuppa and a bacon roll. London's early risers drop by for a breakfast of Maria's famous bubble and squeak. The tea is flowing while the crowds flow over London Bridge.

8am

As the wholesale market closes the trustees' team of 'sweepers' clear the market in preparation for the retail market. Large lorries are replaced by the transit vans and estate cars of the retail market's producers. A few of the wholesalers have turned their hand to retailing.

10am

Producers from all over the country bring a range of fresh produce to the retail market. As with the wholesalers, they travel great distances to get to Borough, some are from the furthest reaches of England, Wales, Scotland and Ireland, others come to London twice a week from such countries as France, Italy, Sweden and Spain. They bring with them all nature of food, including; fish, meat, game and poultry, fruit and vegetables, ciders, cheeses, breads, coffees, cakes and patisseries. Stallholders swap stories and discuss the week's produce as it is unloaded for the day's trading.

12am

2pm

Once everything's ready for the day, the retailers take a break, a coffee and perhaps a pastry – it's a chance for them to prepare themselves for the onslaught of customers who, come rain or shine, are now making their way to Borough for their weekly shopping. At this point the market feels serene, the stalls are like still-lifes, the produce beautifully arranged for the customers to view, but the aisles are strangely quiet. The stage is set, now all that is needed are the players – and their audience.

There's little time to wait. The stallholders are soon doing a roaring trade and there is a lively buzz humming through the market. For the first hour the shoppers tend to be locals buying groceries to take home, but by lunchtime, particularly on a Friday, they mingle with besuited office workers carving their way through the market from Southwark's newly-refurbished warehouse office spaces. For them a trip to the market is a real treat at the end of the working week. They stop by for a tasty lunch-to-go – and maybe for something special to cook for the weekend, too.

4pm

By mid-afternoon the market is heaving with activity. The workers may have returned to their offices but shoppers and tourists from all over London have now arrived to enjoy the spectacle that is Borough Market. The chatter of voices and operatic arias emanating from Kevin Loe, opera singer come grocer, at the Turnips stall, provides a sharp contrast to the relative quiet of the night-time wholesale market.

6pm

Early evening and the retail market is now closed. For a few hours, the cages are silent and the people are gone. But the local pubs, four of which surround the immediate perimeter of the market, are bursting at the seams. Workers, traders, locals and the last of the shoppers have stopped to enjoy the fine ales and food sourced from the market traders. The pubs remain busy until last call. Some have moved on to local restaurants for a more substantial meal. Since the revival of the retail market, new restaurants have sprung up and now mingle comfortably with the old. Most eaters are just signing their bills when the lorries begin to arrive for the commencement of another 24 hour cycle in the life of the Borough Market.

8pm

Market thoughts

Maria Moruzzi, *Proprietor of Maria's Market Café.*

My family's been in the area for 42 years. It used to be my parents' business and as I got older I helped out, as Italian families do. I started around the age of seven. I'd pick up cups, do the washing up, pass toast to people and entertain the customers – brightening up their lives. My family is from Emilia-Romana in Northern Italy. I was born in Kent. I keep telling everyone I'm a belle from the garden of England.

I wanted to do something glamorous. Both of my parents were taken ill, so I ended up helping out for a couple of weeks and those weeks turned into years.

When I was a kid the market was thriving. It was packed with grocery sellers. It was vibrant. They used to 'pull' from Bermondsey Street and when I say 'pull' I mean they used to load up wheelbarrows with produce and pull them all the way to the market. It went on from one in the morning until four in the afternoon.

The market has really cleaned up. The architects have been really sympathetic and have kept the market atmosphere, which is a very hard thing to do. They're very clever because they've actually moved in to the area, so they understand it. I think they really hit it on the nail.

The stallholders love their produce. They've got this passion about their food – that's what the market is really about: passion. And it radiates. Everyone who works here is happy. It's hard work and they come from a very long way but they integrate with the history. The market has become a bit touristy. But tourists come and go. When you get the regulars, they add to the community. The customer and the stallholder become like an extended family.

Bubble is what I'm known for. It's really weird, because bubble originates from the poor East End – it was the poor man's food. If I'm busy my customers help me. You'll find people washing up, serving each other, taking orders, making tea and cleaning tables. It doesn't matter who they are. I like talking. I take time to know the people who come in to my café. By the time they've left I know where they work, what they do, if they're married. I'm not being nosy. It's just that I take an interest.

They filmed Howard's End at the back of the café. When they were finishing the last scene the cameraman packed up his camera and realised he didn't have any film in it. So they had to re-shoot the entire scene. I've met some unusual people: Guy Ritchie, Sean Connery – he came in to use our 'facilities', and Catherine Zeta Jones. It's funny, I never go anywhere, and I have just a little back street café, yet I've met some of the biggest names in show business.

I'm only doing this four days a week: Wednesday, Thursday, Friday and Saturday. The other days are 'my time'. I study Japanese and the computer. I like to show off. I know everything and nothing, me. I speak French and Italian, and regional Parmigiano.

WHOLESALE PRODUCE

There's been a market in Borough for a thousand years. In its heyday the wholesalers numbered more than 250; today there are less than 10 nightly traders bringing their fruit and vegetables to sell, while the rest of London sleeps. These dedicated producers provide more than a valued service; they encapsulate the spirit and soul of the market.

Borough Market may make the headlines today as London's favourite retail market, but it is its historic wholesale trade that has kept it alive over the centuries. The buying and selling of fruit and vegetables has been the mainstay of the business on this site for more than 250 years and still continues throughout the night, six days a week. For many centuries before that, it resided in former premises close by.

Records traced back to AD 1014 show that the market then sold fish, grain and cattle – as well as vegetables, and because of its central location (the meeting points of all roads from the South Coast & Southern Counties into the City of London), merchants from all over Europe would travel from coastal ports to trade at Borough Market.

At the height of the Victorian era most of the food imported to the capital of the British Empire arrived at wharves alongside London Bridge and Tooley Street – hence its name – 'London's Larder', and later on via London Bridge railway station, (the first large railway terminus in Central London). Thousands of tons of produce were wheeled the few yards from the train to the market.

It is now the oldest fruit and vegetable wholesale market still trading from its present 4.5 acre site – since 1756 – in Central London. And today the horse drawn carts, trains and barrows have been replaced by trucks laden with produce from all corners of the UK and many parts of Europe; ready to supply greengrocers, restaurateurs and hotels throughout the South East and Greater London.

The wholesale market has left its mark on the whole area, from the atmospheric warehouse buildings, constructed to store the produce, to the Market Porter pub, formerly known as The Harrow, which still operates a special wholesale market early opening licence.

In its heyday, the wholesale market consisted of around 250 traders filling the entire market premises. Salesman John Stark, known as Jock, who works for Sugarmans, purveyors of fruit and vegetables, has been connected with the market for 35 years. Until seven years ago he was a customer, sourcing produce for his greengrocers in South Nunhead; now he sits on the selling side of the fence. He recalls how, not so long ago, the wholesale trade was a hive of activity, with over 100 wholesale companies in operation, "It was great fun. The porters would have a sports day and race the barrows all the way to Brighton." He also has fond memories of the barrows themselves. "Loading them was a fine art. The porters would stack them with a ton and a half of weight. If they got the balance right they could lift it up, fully loaded, with just two fingers. Get it wrong and everything would go flying at the first bump in the road."

But those glory days are long gone, the barrows replaced by fork lifts. Now just seven remaining companies fit easily into the Jubilee Market alone. The demise of the wholesale trade is due to the arrival and rapid growth of supermarket trade. Despite this significant downturn in the wholesale market's fortunes, the trustees have no intentions of closing it down. The generally held view is that the decline has bottomed-out, as those greengrocers still operating have adapted and by so doing, survived. And, on an optimistic note, there is a growing trend amongst consumers of favouring the smaller, more intimate stores again. Maybe this bodes well for an upturn in the wholesale trade of the future.

Besides, the wholesale and retail trade are still, to some degree, mutually dependent. Most of the wholesalers either have their own retail market stalls, or supply others. Tony Booth, best-known for his wild mushrooms, runs a retail store each Saturday, as does the Chairman of the Tenants' Association, Andrew Sugarman, as well as Turnips, who specialise in produce for the catering trade. In fact, some wholesalers work through the night then set up stall at the retail market to begin a full day's work, first thing in the morning.

A thousand years old, the regeneration project has successfully prepared Borough Market for another thousand years of trading.

MOST OF THE
WHOLESALERS EITHER
HAVE THEIR OWN
RETAIL MARKET STALLS,
OR SUPPLY
OTHERS.

Market thoughts

I started working at the market a few years ago. I'm an opera singer and was looking for a job I could do when I wasn't singing. A friend of a friend told me about Turnips. They're very flexible. I went to America to perform in Bizet's Carmen and they let me disappear for a few months.

Kevin Loe

Opera singer and part-time greengrocer at Turnips.

There are a number of people who sing at Turnips. Most are friends of mine who started after I did. Borough is like a theatre. The stallholders are the performers; the customers the audience. People like to come and be part of the show. You'd never get the same kind of exchange in the aisles of a supermarket.

When I'm working at the market it's like being on stage. It's a licence to show off. I often start singing when I'm working. I love getting a reaction – it's probably why I'm still singing. I have a large voice. It carries far. If you've heard me sing you'd remember.

I've had a lot of jobs from the market. I've sung at people's weddings. Jamie Oliver asked me to sing at the christening of his daughter, Poppy. Jamie comes to the market a lot. He came in earlier this year and showed me Poppy as I hadn't seen her for a while. Man she has some hair.

London can be a bit of a drab city sometimes, but the market brings it to life. It brings colour to London. I was born in Africa, in Zimbabwe. My parents moved here when I was quite young.

I grew up in East London. So going south of the river was always out of the question. Nobody from the East End goes south of the river. I suppose you could say working in the market has opened my eyes to a new part of London.

I couldn't recognize half the fruit and vegetables when I started and now I'm telling customers what things are. For example, people on the whole don't know what salsify is. It's not just a dirty stick. It's a really nice root vegetable and it's very easy to cook.

People are afraid to eat white asparagus. So I try to persuade them to try new things.

Things like artichokes are ridiculously easy to cook. People are quite open to buying new things if you suggest them.

I think Borough Market is inspiring the supermarkets. You're starting to see a lot of fruit and vegetables in supermarkets that were once only sold in places like Borough Market.

Some people complain that the market is too expensive but if you can taste the difference – it's made supermarkets change their tune.

Shopping at the market is fun. If you want to squeeze something, you can squeeze it. If you want to taste something, you can taste it. If you don't know what something is, you ask.

SOURCE TO STALL

BY DOMINIC MURPHY

Traceability is key to the produce on sale at the Borough Market. And the food has been vetted for quality before it even reaches the stalls. The dedicated traders at Borough's bi-weekly retail market make the journey from across the country and around the globe, all with the same intention: to bring the best food in the world to London's Larder.

It's 11.30 on a Thursday night and Peter Gott is crossing London Bridge on the last leg of his drive from Cumbria. He has been on the road for more than six hours and soon he'll be unloading the week's meat into the fridges behind his Borough Market stall. Sometimes he squeezes in a drop to a restaurant before he packs up for the night, at Jamie Oliver's Fifteen, say, or St John, in Farringdon across the Thames, but tonight there are no deliveries planned. If he's lucky he'll be in bed by 1am, catching some sleep before the six o'clock start on Friday morning. "I've just taken on a small flat," he says. "Before that, it was a mattress in a van: we slept rough." Like Gott, between 75 and 100 stallholders make the weekly journey to market on Thursday night and Friday morning, for two days of hectic trading. Their customers range from the connoisseur to the plain curious, from restaurateurs stocking up for the weekend to tourists who are here on recommendation. For some – customers and stallholders – Borough is a pilgrimage: these people really care about food. And for many, these 48 hours are their lifeblood, bringing what is often a small volume, niche product to a market of some 20,000 people each week.

The exact number of traders depends on the time of year (the run up to Christmas is busy), availability of seasonal produce and the weather (would you want to stand outside all day in freezing February rain?). There are producers displaying a single line, and aggregators bringing in produce from several farms. There is meat, fish, fruit, veg, flowers, deli produce and snacks: ostrich burgers for a touch of the exotic, bubble and squeak for old time's sake.

There are traders from all parts of the country, produce from all around the globe. It's paradise for a listmaker. Beef and dairy from the West Country, oysters from Essex, gravadlax from Scandinavia, teas from Japan, cheese from South Wales, charcuterie from Germany and Spain. There are chocolates made in the teeming heart of London, and scallops caught by divers off the Dorset coast. There's even seaweed brought over from the west coast of Ireland.

What these traders have in common is not only a dedication to quality food, but also the distinctiveness of their produce and how it reflects the region from where it came. Gott's speciality is pig: all manner of pork products, including pies that have become a Borough legend. He keeps 250 rare breeds on his 60-acre farm near Kendal, in the Lake District (Tamworth, Middle White, Saddleback, British Lop ...) and a further 120 of their hairy cousins, wild boar. Crucially, says Gott, all of them live outdoors. The boar even have 19 acres of woodland in which to forage, just as if they were in the wild.

Often to be seen in a bowler hat and plus-fours, Gott looks like a nineteenth-century gentleman butcher. He could have featured in an old Punch cartoon, maybe had a walk-on part in *Middlemarch*. But there are no gimmicks, he says, when it comes to his pork. Get him started and he's riffing about the additives in normal meat, how pigs are reared mostly indoors and under intensive conditions by farmers that put profit before quality. This, he says, not only has the possible knock-on effect to human health, but definitely affects taste. "It sounds corny, but we do produce good food – food with integrity. I can tell you exactly what is in the sausages." The fact that customers at Borough are meeting the producers is important, too. "What's never valued in markets is the social interaction, the integrity," he stresses, "If someone came back to me and said that one of my

BEEF AND DAIRY FROM
THE WEST COUNTRY, OYSTERS FROM ESSEX,
GRAVADLAX FROM SCANDINAVIA,
TEAS FROM JAPAN, CHEESE
FROM SOUTH WALES,
CHARCUTERIE FROM GERMANY AND SPAIN.

sausages was crap, then it hits me in the pocket and I'll do something about it."

Gott was here at the beginning when a handful of traders would brave any weather for the monthly market that preceded today's twice weekly affair. They gritted their teeth on those grim winter mornings, and tried to keep up their spirits. Sometimes, "we wondered if we were right in the head." Word got around, and more traders and punters began to turn up. But who could have guessed it would become what you see today.

Another Cumbrian who has watched the market blossom is Andrew Sharp. Sharp breeds Herdwick sheep, a distinctive upland beast that probably came over with the Vikings. From these, his produce includes mutton salamis and air-dried mutton – "think Spanish-style prosciutto," he says, but one where the raw material has come from pastures in the Lake District. Yes, you heard right. Sharp sells mutton – a meat that spawned sexist jokes and probably had its last outing as a legitimate foodstuff in the time of *Oliver Twist*. And the fact that he can shift the stuff at a premium price is a measure of how sophisticated our food industry has become, and, to some extent, the respect that Borough confers.

A handful of years ago, to call your product mutton would have been the kiss of death, the way to ensure you got no purchasers. The word conjured up a beast that was past its sell by date, one that was only good for the knackers. Why buy mutton when you could get tender, juicy lamb? Why buy mutton, come to think of it, when anything else would do? But there's mutton and there's mutton, says Sharp. "We have 200 odd breeds of sheep in the UK and they're not all the same thing. If you've got a modern breed like Belltex it's very Arnold Schwarzenegger in shape but very coarse to eat. They're about three times the size of a Herdwick but because they grow fast they don't have the same quality: it's like trees, the longer it takes to mature, the better the quality of wood."

Sharp's relationship with Borough has done more than raise the profile of a breed of sheep, though. Crucially, he drives down the produce of other small livestock farmers to the market, and customers are prepared to pay for quality. These farmers could well face bankruptcy if they tried to compete with large producers who can survive on the narrow margins offered by the supermarkets. And the economic benefits of this co-operative system can be seen in the price of the local sheep. "When we started in London five or six years ago, a Herdwick lamb was worth 16 quid," says Sharp. "Now they're worth £58."

At the other end of the country, beneath chalkland downs in the Arreton Valley, is the home of Isle of Wight Tomatoes. Here, says the company's Jeff MacDonald, they enjoy a micro-climate. Few things, he argues, could better capture the characteristics of the island than the humble tomato. "We have one per cent more sunshine than the rest of the country, the valley is a suntrap," he says. "I tell people it's like a mini Rioja in Spain."

Sunshine, says MacDonald, has a massive influence on flavour. One of the reasons so many tomatoes taste of nothing, he says, is they are picked before they are ripe. This gives the large producers more time to get them to the supermarket. "If they'd been left on the plant and allowed to ripen naturally, then everyone would be happy," he says, "But if they're picked early when they're orange, packed, refrigerated, put on a lorry, unloaded from a lorry, then they could have been

around for at least two weeks before you buy them."

At Borough, says MacDonald, when you buy one of his tomatoes, it will have been harvested in the previous 24 hours or, at the most, the day before that. It will have caught the 4am ferry from the island and been driven up the same day that you buy it. And strange though this may sound to anyone familiar with our weather, they taste of the English sunshine. There are around 10 varieties that come up to Borough each week and the other farmers markets MacDonald supplies around the capital. These range from a classic Beefsteak and the medium-sized Elegance, to more exotic varieties such as the stripy Red Zebra, White Wonder and Black Prince. Again unlike the supermarkets, says MacDonald, perfection of shape and size is not guaranteed: "they do get a fresh product, but there are the odd sized ones, ones with a scar on, the extra green tomato attached to the vine. You get the tomato that was picked." It's a small price to pay for flavour.

Take the ferry from the Isle of Wight, across the Solent to the mainland, head in the opposite direction to London, and you'll soon arrive in Dorset, home of Long Crichel Bakery. The business was set up four years ago by Jamie and Rose Campbell, not as a result of some driving vocation for early morning graft at the bread oven, but more as a pleasant thing to do from their Wimborne home.

"I've always been interested in bread but I'm not by profession a baker," says Jamie. "I'm an architect, my wife is an architect. But we've both got family backgrounds in catering. We've got quite a lot of space here and we thought, 'what are we going to do with it?' And then we thought, why don't we start a bakery. It was as idiotic as that." Long Crichel specialises in French 'artisanal' bread – that is,

robust traditional peasant loaves that predate the arrival of the poncey modern baguette and croissant, or 'Viennoiserie', to France in the late nineteenth century. The bakery makes nine types of loaf in a traditional wood-fired oven; all of them organic, six of which are sourdoughs. (Put simply, this means a particular day's batch of bread being made using some dough produced from the day before as the raising agent.)

Unlike the Cumbrian farmers and numerous other Borough traders, there is nothing traditional to Dorset in what the Campbells do – they learned their craft from a French baker they befriended when living near Tours. But their bread is a characteristic product that nonetheless bears the mark of the region it comes from. Sourdoughs are based on wild yeast, says Jamie, and that which you will be eating in a Long Crichel loaf comes from the Campbells' own vine – grapes that had begun to rot with the resulting bloom used to make a yeast. Also, the organic flour they use is from a local mill up the road in Shaftesbury. And the Campbells are not simply repeating the original French recipes, but have adapted them to give a distinctive Long Crichel product.

Like the Campbells, Jill Mead and Steve Benbow came to be trading at Borough almost by accident. Not that they had to go very far to get there. They live just across the road, near London Bridge. And their distinctive, regional product that bears the mark of their metropolitan home? Honey. From London bees. It started with one hive on the roof of the block of flats where they live. From here, you can see across the river to the city's financial heart, which is perhaps why they decided to turn the roof into a garden, an escape from the concrete, steel and glass that is

THERE IS MEAT, FISH, FRUIT, VEG, FLOWERS, DELI PRODUCE AND SNACKS: OSTRICH BURGERS FOR A TOUCH OF THE EXOTIC, BUBBLE AND SQUEAK FOR OLD TIME'S SAKE.

all around. "We started up the business four or five years ago," says Mead. "Stevie and I are both from the countryside. We have a huge yearning not to be in London and we thought we'd bring the country in."

Mead and Benbow are both photographers, and it was their profession that drew them to London in the first place, she from North Yorkshire, he from Shropshire. Both of them, says Mead, had photographed beekeepers on separate occasions and something about these people touched a nerve. "One day, we thought it would be nice to have bees up there – we'd have chickens if we could get away with it. We put a hive behind the lift shaft and got the most amazing yield in the first year." The resulting business, the London Honey Company, was, "more of a part-time hobby that got completely out of hand".

Inspired by the success of their initial effort, Mead and Benbow started to look for other sites for hives. Although beekeeping conjures images of an idyllic countryside lifestyle, in reality, says Mead, London is the perfect place to keep them. "Whereas a lot of beekeepers have to move their bees around to follow the pollen, you don't have to do that in the city." There is an amazing diversity of flowers packed into small gardens, allotments, parks and along canals, which keeps the pollen supply more or less continuous. "And people wonder whether it's dodgy, full of lead and things, but we had it tested and it was fine."

Eventually, after contacting several electricity boards, they negotiated the use of some wasteland around a disused generating station in Woolwich, where they kept most of their hives until they were vandalised last year. After this setback, they advertised for people with gardens who would be prepared to host their hives, and

were overwhelmed by the response. "We could have had bees in every postcode, it was ridiculous the amount of interest we got," says Mead. "But we realised that we needed a bulk in one place – around April, May, June you have to be really on top of the bees. It's around this time they might swarm, and you don't want that in London." The couple now have most of their hives at the Wetland Centre, in leafy Barnes, further down the Thames. Here, the bees are allowed to stay rent free in return for occasional beekeeping demonstrations to the general public, and the occasional pot of honey. "We do give the bees a holiday sometimes," says Mead. "We take the hives down to Dungeness for the wood sage in June. What we get from that is probably our best honey."

While the likes of the London Honey Company and Long Crichel Bakery are fledgling businesses, that of Essex Oysterman owner Richard Haward has been in the family for generations. As the name suggests, Haward produces Colchester native oysters, a shellfish found around the coastal inlets of Haward's home in West Mersea, Essex. "We have a section of one of the creeks," he says. "My family has owned it for more than 60 years and they worked it before that. There have been oyster beds here for 200 years."

West Mersea is one of the few places you can find the Colchester native oyster which, says Haward, gets a distinctive flavour from the marshes that drain into the oyster beds. And contrary to the popular notion that you should always swallow these molluscs down in one, Haward recommends savouring the flavour. "A good native oyster is a very firm thing that you can bite and you're biting something solid," he says. "It's a waste just to swallow it without getting some of the taste."

The Colchester native oysters are in season from September to March, but Haward also grows wild rock oysters, originally from the Pacific, which are available year-round. On any given week, his catch is usually in purification tanks on Tuesdays and Wednesdays, ready to be driven to market packed in seaweed at 6am on Fridays and Saturdays. Borough Market, says Haward, is his main outlet – restaurants buy from him, as well as regular punters and tourists who might only want to sample one of these shellfish. But he is keen to spread the net wider – and bring what he sees as an undiscovered indigenous food to a wider public. At the moment, he argues, people are reluctant to experiment if they have never had oysters. You tend to be only able to buy them by the half dozen, particularly in restaurants. "And people don't want to do that in case they don't like them."

The French cheese specialists Marie and Franck Le Blais have never had any problems persuading British people to experiment. The meat and two veg English do not exactly have a reputation for adventurous tastes, but, according to Marie, we love smelly cheese. "We were very surprised at the beginning," she says of their early experience at Borough. "We thought that the English didn't like mature cheese, but they do." Very popular is Époisses, from Burgundy, a cheese which, she says, is both, "very strong and very smelly."

The Le Blais run Pays d'Auge Fromages, and have been coming to the market for the past two years. They sell cheese from all over France – Camembert and Livarot from Normandy, Tomme de Chevre from the Pyrenees. Twice a month, Franck drives to Normandy and the big national market at Rungis, near Orly airport in Paris, to stock up. "We don't have any industrial cheeses," says Marie. "We sell mainly raw milk – not pasteurised – cheese from small producers."

Personal contact with farmers is important, she says. You have to know who made the cheese and its characteristics for customers back in London.

There are favourites among the British punters that are the staples of their business – Valençay from the Loire, a goat's cheese creamy at the edges and firmer inside; Gruyère from Savoire in the Alps; and Brie de Meaux, a creamy, fresher variety of the famous cheese. But the Le Blais occasionally stumble across an obscure regional gem. "This summer we went on holiday to Ile de Re and we met someone who just makes goat's cheese near La Rochelle," says Marie. This cheese has a unique salty taste because of the tidal salt or fleur de sel on the marshes upon which the animals graze. Expect to see it soon in SE1.

This is one of the real thrills of the Borough scene – often little-known regional produce finding its way to the heart of London; the sort of thing you might come across on holiday and think, ooh, I wish I could buy some of that at home. Another is the sheer variety of food on offer, the anything-goes-so-long-as-it's-quality approach: sun-dried tomatoes prepared the same way for generations, under the same roof as new-fangled seaweed pasta. The supermarkets, from whom we buy most of our food, make honourable attempts to emulate this situation, but the scale of their needs means only big suppliers get a look in. And when food manufacture moves towards such industrial quantities, it's the little guy making the one-off product who feels the pinch. Borough Market helps sustain these small producers, and in some cases, prevent a way of life from dying out. It is a David to the supermarkets' Goliath. And one with exceedingly good taste.

Market thoughts

Henrietta Green
*Author of The Food Lovers'
Guide to Britain.*

It was a bold, exciting Friday – a Friday in 1998 that changed the face of food and food shopping in the UK. That Friday was the day I held my Food Lovers' Fair at Borough Market. When I first came up with the idea of the fairs the producers just weren't interested, I couldn't get the farmers to come. They didn't seem to understand what I was trying to do. Frankly, back then I had no idea what it would be like, or if anyone would come. But they did – in their thousands.

I was inspired in New York City. I went there in the late '80s and something serious was happening. I could feel the winds of change. Farmers' markets were emerging.

It had to happen here. London desperately needed something like Borough Market. It has sparked a food revolution that has spread through the country. We were way ahead of our time.

'Where is it?' That's what I famously remarked when Randolph Hodgson from Neal's Yard Dairy told me about Borough Market. He's the one who suggested I hold a Food Lovers' Fair there.

Many stallholders sold out on the first day and had to go back to their farms to stock up for the rest of the weekend, as the first market ran right through from Friday to Sunday.

"Is it you I have to blame for the worst weekend of my life?" That's what one couple asked me. I think they made a total of five trips and spent £600 on quality produce.

It is not enough to pay lip service. You can't go to the supermarket and then whinge about there not being good markets, or fishmongers and butchers. Every purchase we make has its implications. We should all remember the power of the purse and shop accordingly.

People go to markets on holiday. It's a pleasurable experience, but they don't associate it with everyday life. Back home they think of shopping as a chore that needs to be done as quickly as possible. And end up going to supermarkets.

Supermarket food is sanitised. Consumers think of the white, neon light, bright, airless, windowless supermarket as somewhere in which they are being looked after. They feel what they buy there is safe. But is it? The food lacks so much – taste, texture and character to start.

There are some equations consumers just don't make. If you have two chickens costing £1.99 and £6.99 respectively, people probably think the higher prices are about frills, not what must have been done or sacrificed in terms of rearing to make the other so cheap.

People who go to Borough Market have lost their fear of food. They've learned to trust and question and have woken up to the fact that there are British farmers who produce with love and care. Perhaps they should question the other things they buy too – clothes, for example. Where and how have they been produced? Maybe the food revolution will make people look at this and other aspects of their lives.

RETAIL
PRODUCE

BY HENRIETTA GREEN

Shopping is the key to successful cooking, for without good produce you don't stand a chance. In recent years we have moved back to simpler methods, where quality really shines through. Where better than the Borough Market to source the ingredients, with the producers on hand to provide you with all the essential facts about their food.

I started my flirtation with markets one long, hot summer when I was just five and on holiday with my family on France's Cote d'Azur. Most mornings Caroline, the cook, and I would trudge down the road to the 'Marche Municipale' by the port in Cannes, armed with our battered baskets. I was captivated by the sights, sounds and smells. I had entered a new world and embarked on a relationship that has lasted a lifetime. Since then I have visited or worked in markets all around the world – from Stroud to Sydney, Notting Hill to New York, taking in points in between – but Borough still proves one of the most alluring. I first met it when it operated purely as a wholesale market. During the day you would have thought it a wallflower, quiet and unnoticed: it did attract visitors but they came during the unsociable, early morning hours, eagerly buying for restaurants or shops. As most of us were leaving the warm comfort of our beds, Borough was closing down for the day.

Just as the princess was kissed awake from a long slumber, I like to think that it was my three-day Food Lovers' Fair in 1998 that awoke Borough and brought it to the public's consciousness. At the initiative of Southwark Festival there we were, on that Friday morning, 50 stallholders – all British speciality food producers whom I had hand-picked and vetted – lined up and eager to start selling. Some, such as Furness Fish, The Ginger Pig and Wild Beef, are now market regulars; others, such as De Gustibus or The Monmouth Coffee Company, even have shops surrounding the market. Back then it was very different, as several stallholders had hardly sold direct to the public before. Mrs Elizabeth King, whose handmade pork pies are justly sought after every week, had only been at one county show previously, as had Wendy Brandon with her sumptuously fruity jams. Inexperience was coupled with an unforgettable fear that first morning. "Will anyone come?" was all I could think in a

sheer panic of anxiety. Thankfully, I was worrying needlessly. By noon several stalls had already sold out and if I had had 50p every time a shopper came up to tell me this is how they wanted to shop for ever more, I would have made my fortune.

It would be too easy to say the rest is history, as it has been a long hard struggle for all the producers, with several steep learning curves along the route. Running a market, as I know only too well, is not easy, but it is immensely satisfying. A vibrant, successful one like Borough generates energy, excitement and sheer pleasure. Going there on Market Day for a shop is not unlike going on a date, with a similar sense of attraction and thrill of the chase. Whether it is Peter Gott of Sillfield Farm urging you in to his stall to buy his sausages or Jan McCourt of Northfield Farm to buy his, you realise that – whether they know it or not – they are flirting away, doing their best to 'attract' us to their stalls. It's all part of the game.

Compare that to the joyless, anonymous experience of your supermarket. At Borough there is charm, bustle, a human scale, approachability and friendliness.

Of course, if the food were not good – or even better than most – no one would bother to go. It may be satisfying to have human contact but it is worthless unless coupled with quality and authenticity. The producers who come to Borough are predominantly craft producers, or as the French would call them, "artisanal", who work on a small scale. Their produce tends to be farmed or grown extensively and sustainably with livestock farmed according to welfare-friendly standards, so what you might expect to find is distinctive produce that celebrates our regional diversity. Take meat for example, at Borough you will find several of our traditional, native and rare-breeds and because the emphasis here is on taste and flavour, they will have been slow grown and properly hung.

Whether talking about primary produce such as meat or processed food such as cheese, bread, cakes and so on, it is important to emphasise that quality is a chain and that all the relevant links need to be in place. Take a piece of farmhouse cheese; its eating qualities will be influenced not only by the actual milk (the raw ingredients) but also by how it is made, matured and stored. At Borough, what you find is food made with love, care and attention to detail, with flavour and personality. And if you have shopped at supermarkets where you have become accustomed to a bland diet, this may come as a surprise. Think of Borough, if you like, as a dating agency. It puts us, the consumers in touch with them, the producers and offers the opportunity for us to meet one another face to face. At Borough we will be served by people who know about the food they are selling. So they'll be able to answer our questions and address our concerns. They can furnish us with the all-important detailed information on the how, what, when and where of their produce. And the more we know, the more empowered we will be, the more able to make informed choices about the food we buy. For those of us who care about traceability, sustainability, animal welfare, chemical inputs, additives and all the other issues around food production, knowledge is the key. The producers also benefit by not only reaching their market and cutting out the middle man, but they can also find out what we really want and thus, serve our needs or desires. At Borough the stallholders can provide you with details of every stage of their product's cycle. With meat, for example, the chances are they have reared, hung and butchered it themselves. Borough is unique. My dream for Britain would be that every city and town has its own Borough, but for now I have to content myself that at least London has its larder. So go, shop, make the connections, buy the food.

Market thoughts

Randolph Hodgson
Founder and owner of Neal's Yard Dairy.

I needed a job. That's how I ended up working in the cheese industry. After finishing a degree course in food science at London University, I applied for a summer job to help make cheese at a whole-food shop in Neal's Yard.

I was working for a guy called Nicholas Saunders. He set up Neal's Yard Dairy in 1979. He used to call in a lady who ran the neigbouring coffee shop to sample the cheese. I used to say, "Oh, no, not that fierce woman again." Now she's my wife.

One of our first customers was John Cleese. He dropped in to buy some cheese, but I was still learning how to make it. All we had was some yogurt, so it all rather descended into a Monty Python sketch.

I've been coming to Borough for over 20 years. I knew it as my first wholesale customer was in Cathedral Street. We moved in more than a year before the Food Lovers' Fair. Our shop in Covent Garden was very busy and we needed a space to store cheese and run our wholesale business from. The choices were either a modern industrial estate or something with atmosphere.

I love markets and loved the area. It was a natural place for us to be but the shop in Covent Garden was purpose-built to retail cheese. Borough was designed for storage. As a result it's a little chaotic – we didn't expect to be so busy.

Farmhouse cheeses in Britain and Ireland are returning from the brink of extinction. There are many skilled cheesemakers in the UK and Ireland but they really didn't have a market before.

In Britain we still have a more utilitarian view of food as fuel. This is not because we lack the palate or the interest. The interest is there but the opportunity to express it isn't.

Borough Market gives consumers an opportunity to taste and compare and learn. This will increase the demand for good food and then more will become available. Cheese in supermarkets has improved hugely over the past 10 years. Supermarkets are part of the revolution to better food – they're just not leading it.

I love the architectural evolution of the market. There's been a unique mixture of individuals and events. The fact that our shop opened before the regeneration has meant the way our business was operating lead the design rather than the other way round. The vision of George Nicholson and Ken Greig has been perfect.

My favourite cheese changes every day. It is important to realise that cheese varies a lot from batch to batch. You must taste it before you buy anything. I have a soft spot for the traditional varieties: Lancashire, Cheshire, Stilton and Cheddar.

I don't have a specific way of eating cheese. It is often a snack food – fast food, in fact.

MEAT, GAME & POULTRY

Where meat, game and poultry are concerned, breed, feed, age, welfare regime, medication, slaughtering, hanging and butchering will all affect the quality of the end product. At the Borough Market it is common for the stallholders to have overseen the entire process themselves – and you'll find them all proud to share in their knowledge.

BEEF Borough offers the opportunity to buy some of our traditional British breeds of beef. With its wide range of butchers it is unique that under one roof you can see so many different breeds – and have the chance to discuss their qualities. So look out for Hereford Red Devon and White Park, which bring history to your plate. There's a good reason to encourage this. Quality is a chain and every link of that chain has to be in place, starting with the breed, how it's fed, reared, sent to slaughter, hung, stored and butchered. All these things are going to affect the quality – no one factor should be isolated.

As hanging improves the texture and flavour of beef it's particularly important that it should be well hung. Insist on a minimum of 15 days although some stallholders will hang for as long as 30. Remember, although most people think the flesh should be a vivid red, the colour of fresh blood, it is not necessarily a sign of good quality. Some of the best beef I have ever bought has been a much darker, deeper red, a sign that it's been well and truly hung. Look for a firm, slightly moist piece of flesh with a clean aroma and layer of glossy fat, the colour of which, depending on the breed, can vary from a milky white to a buttery yellow.

Market thoughts

Iqbal Wahhab
Restaurateur and proprietor of Roast restaurant in the Floral Hall.

The timing was perfect for what the trustees were planning in terms of the revival of Britain's oldest food market and my own plans to create a restaurant dedicated to the best of British cooking and British farming.

I now live very close by. I often return home from shopping there and look at all the goodies I've bought then realise I need to go back for more because nothing I've got goes with anything else.

British food has been viewed as unfashionable – especially among younger people – because that's what you ate at home and the more glamorous lure of dining out meant the lure of foreign food.

Food trends are incredibly difficult to predict but there does seem to be a movement away from fussy, over-garnished haute cuisine, which is a relief. I ran a couple of magazines about Indian food. We would quote the famous surveys indicating that curry had taken over from fish and chips as the nation's favourite food. It made for great headlines but it had an unpredicted consequence; it played straight into the hands of the practitioners of the great British sport of self-deprecation.

I have lived in Britain most of my life but being of Asian origin allows me the chance to dip in and out of an entirely British perspective. I don't think it's a coincidence that it's taken someone who's not entirely British to have the confidence to be able to say: "British food doesn't have to be perceived this way."

Roast was formed out of an attitude, rather than a straightforward commercially-driven perspective. Its aim is to make a point about British cooking and producers. My family arrived in Britain from Bangladesh in 1964. My brother was five and my sister nine. I was eight months old! So everyone else had a Bengali diet, but as a child I had some trouble coming to grips with a wholly spiced diet, so I was the kid who loved school dinners.

I've been devouring books on British food. I'm fascinated by the history but also by the breadth and depth of the British culinary repertoire that has fallen by the wayside. A good restaurant will lead as well as reflect public tastes. The public looks more closely at what restaurateurs and chefs stand for and promote. In turn, we take a greater responsibility and duty of care over what it is we say and do because a more knowledgeable public is also a less forgiving one.

British cooking has been looking too far forward. Chefs of modern British restaurants have been too eager to use non-British techniques and ingredients because they don't feel they can put their name to a dish unless they've messed with it.

My wish is for people to be proud of their national cuisine but we don't expect customers to finish their meals at Roast with a resounding chorus from Land of Hope and Glory.

63

Pan-fried Sirloin Steak with Wild Mushrooms

Serves four

Throughout the autumn at Borough you can buy an amazing range of mushrooms – wild and cultivated. Their earthy flavours really do complement beef. When buying, look for a variety of shapes and colours and use garlic and herbs to accentuate their taste.

4 x sirloin steaks 190gm / 7oz each
550gm / 1lb 4oz mixed wild
    mushrooms
50gm / 2oz chopped shallot
2 cloves garlic, crushed
2 sprigs of thyme
25gm / 1oz chopped flat leaf parsley
75ml / 3floz port
75gm / 3oz unsalted butter
25ml / 1floz olive oil
salt and freshly ground black pepper

1 Remove the steaks from the fridge 20 minutes before cooking so they come up to room temperature.

2 Take the selection of wild mushrooms and scrape off any visible earth with a small knife. Cut into similar sizes and wash in a bowl of cold water, with a pinch of salt. Drain and pat dry in a tea towel.

3 Heat a large frying pan on top of the stove with the oil until it is just starting to smoke, season both sides of the steak and seal quickly, then cook to the desired degree. Remove from the pan and rest for 10 mins in a warm place.

4 Pour off excess fat from the pan. Add 25gm /1oz of the butter and shallots, then soften over a low heat without colouring. Increase the heat, add the mushrooms, garlic and thyme, season with salt and pepper.

5 Once the mushrooms have wilted add the port, scraping the bottom of the pan to incorporate the sediment. Stir in the remainder of the butter to blend the juices with the mushrooms. Add the chopped parsley and serve with the steak.

JOHN TORODE
IN MY BASKET

Creator and chef of Smith's of Smithfield, a four-storey restaurant in London's Smithfield Market, John grew up on a farm in Australia which, he says, gave him a deep passion for properly grown food from an early age.

How often do you go to Borough Market?
I try to get down to the market every week, whether it's to buy some produce or to eat a chorizo in a bun from Brindisa.

What do you buy?
Oh god, where do I start? I always buy bread, some with toppings to munch on and some for home. My boys always spot a sweet or savoury treat. I buy lots of pulses from Brindisa. I get beef from Juan at Rutland and Herdwick lamb from Andrew Sharp. I love the taleggio from the good-looking Italian guys and the crabs from Shellseekers. Flowers are a must. If the boys are with me, we munch on brownies and bags of apples. It changes every time – I'll buy mushrooms if they're around, oysters and maybe some butter or Isle of Wight tomatoes. I love the oatcakes from Neal's Yard and Stinking Bishop if it's really stinking.

What's your favourite product?
I love pork. I make lots of pies and tarts and marinated ribs and slow cooked belly and Thai curry of shoulder. I like simple grilled chops with ambrosia and fried pork with salty duck eggs.

To you, what's most significant about the re-emergence of markets like Borough?
The farmers and producers can sell fantastic food and make a living without having to succumb to the pressure of supplying a supermarket.

How do you think Borough compares to other markets in the world?
Markets around the world have been set up with the idea of servicing the locals and the community, but Borough Market brings people from miles. I live in Streatham, which is six miles away, and when I go, I meet my friend who lives in Queen's Park, which isn't exactly around the corner from Borough.

Has Borough Market introduced you to ingredients you hadn't come across before?
Not really, but it has been a real education for my kids. It's mind blowing – I've been able to show them whole venison, birds with the feathers still on them, real fish and properly cured hams.

Did you go to food markets as a child?
I grew up in a small town in Australia where we had farms all around. However, every week a fruit and vegetable man came to our house in an open flat bed truck with his wares and a pair of scales. The same would happen with the butcher and fishmonger. I started going to markets a bit later in life.

If you could have your own stall at Borough Market, what would you sell?
It would have to be a Portuguese coffee shop with grumpy old men and ladies who smoke a lot. I'd sell coffee, little cakes, and a selection of great wine. I would also have a big tasting table.

Anything else to add?
Now I am hungry!

tip My chips are cooked in nothing but dripping. It imparts a delicious, rich flavour. Potatoes – and other root veggies – were made for it. Our dripping is quite popular with small households who want the dripping without making an entire roast. David Kitson, Farmhouse Direct

tip Texture and colour are important when you're buying beef. Our cattle feed only on grass, resulting in meat with a grain that's so fine you can eat it raw. Ideally, this is what you want; along with a dark colouring – this signifies that it's been hung longer. Richard Vines, Wild Beef

PORK

If once pork were avoided in summer due to lack of refrigeration, nowadays it is a meat for all seasons. The pig is the most efficient of our domesticated animals, as not one jot goes to waste, even its bristles are used for brushes. Traditionally, pigs were reared on farms where cheese was made, as they were fed on the whey, a by-product of cheesemaking. The breeds were good old-fashioned ones, classified as rare breeds, such as Gloucester Old Spot, Saddleback, Tamworth Red and British Lop. Look out for these at the market, as their flavour can be superb. Select meat which is finely grained and pale in colour, without any blemishes and neither too dry nor too wet.

tip **Over the past 25 years a number of rare breeds have disappeared due to intensive farming. Rare breeds are slow to mature and have fewer babies. They're more expensive to rear and produce less. But the pigs have a better life and the result is a better product.** Peter Gott, Sillfield Farm

tip **People have forgotten how tasty a traditional product like faggots – a blend of minced pork belly, pig's liver, sage and onion – can be. Roast them for an hour, then use the juices to make onion gravy. Pour this over the faggots and cook a bit longer – delicious!** Jan McCourt, Northfield Farm

Market thoughts

Peter Gott

Owner of Sillfield Farm in Cumbria, and a Borough stallholder.

I've been farming for 30 years. My speciality is rearing rare-breed pigs such as Gloucester Old Spots, Large White-Middle White crosses, Saddlebacks, which are black with a white girth stripe, and Tamworth crosses; as well as wild boar, which is my real passion.

The Second World War killed the food industry. When mass production and supermarkets came along, we started losing our rare breed pigs and our specialist cheeses.

I was invited to Borough Market in November 1998 by Henrietta Green, to do a Food Lovers' Fair. The retail market spawned from there. We were desperate at the start. To attract customers, we drew up a blackboard with the words 'Borough Market' on it and strapped it to the traffic lights on London Bridge. It was there for three months before someone, probably the police, took it down.

Reality in the city is far removed from the countryside. The market has really introduced city people to seasonality.

Until recently, you were better off eating prison meals than you were school dinners. You have to remember that prisoners were responsible for growing their own food.

Intensive farming forces animals to become machines. Take pigs for example: an intensely farmed pig has up to 24 babies in a year. Her body cannot cope with that.

Sociology is a very important part of market life. Interacting with customers helps us understand what they want, and them understand more about the food they eat.

Supermarkets are watching what we are doing. The market is helping to bring an end to bad production practices. The rise of the fussy consumer should be celebrated. People are becoming more demanding. Great! It means the farmers will work harder to ensure the best possible product is achieved.

Everyone on the Borough Market food committee is a market trader, staff or a trustee. The food committee vets all the applications that come in for people who want to trade in the market. If someone wants to sell muffins at the market, the food committee will ask them: what sort of flour are you using? How long have you been producing this product? What makes it unique?

If every catering company in the country bought British the farming crisis wouldn't exist. As it is, no one can tell you where the food that you're eating has come from. The consumer has a right to know what's on the menu, where it's from and how it was raised.

If I could be remembered for one thing it would be passion. I do it for a craic really.

Pan-fried Pork Loin Chops with Cider Mustard Sauce
Serves four

The flavour and textures of succulent pork chops are perfectly balanced with cider-sweetened mustard, deliciously thickened with the best double cream.

4 x 190gm / 7oz pork chops, trimmed with a 1cm / ½ inch covering of fat around the meat
25ml / 1floz olive oil
25gm / 1oz unsalted butter
sprig of rosemary
2 cloves of garlic, crushed
50ml / 2floz dry cider
150ml / 5floz double cream
50 gm / 2oz grain cider mustard
salt and freshly ground black pepper

1 Slash the fat on the chops at 1 cm / ½ inch intervals to help it melt and crispen during cooking. Now take a frying pan large enough to hold all of the chops, add the oil, butter, garlic and the sprig of rosemary.

2 Season the chops on both sides and fry on one side for 2-3 minutes.

3 Reduce the heat slightly; turn the meat and cook for a further 5-7 minutes, basting with the cooking fat. (To test if the meat is cooked insert a knife next to the bone, when ready the juices should run clear.)

4 Remove the chops from the pan and keep warm. Then pour away half of the fat and add the cider. Turn up the heat and reduce by half, stirring constantly.

5 Add the cream and reduce the sauce until it coats the back of a spoon.

6 Remove from the heat and stir in the mustard, check the seasoning for taste.

7 Pour the sauce over the chops and serve.

FARMER SHARPS
MATURE
HERDWICK
WETHER
LEG

£5.00lb
£11.00kg

LAMB

Lamb is probably the meat that has most retained its seasonal and regional identity. Age, feed and breed all make a difference to its taste. Milk-fed lambs taken from the ewe while still suckling have pale-coloured soft and buttery flesh with a gentle flavour not unlike a creamy rice pudding. They are rarely sold this young in Britain but in France and Spain they are rightly considered a treat. Mutton, on the other hand, is about two years' old and has dark dense flesh with a strong, almost cloying flavour, which can be so rich it needs a sharp vinegar or wine-based sauce to set it off.

Most of our British lamb is fed on grass, giving it a well-rounded flavour, sometimes, however, you can buy Shetland lamb whose diet consists predominantly of heather, or Romney Marsh lamb which graze on fields, watered with sea mists, giving them a pronounced taste. Look out for the salt marsh lamb from Wales and the northwest coast of England. From further north, the hills and fells of Cumbria, comes Herdwick lamb with its pungent, aromatic flavour.

Two factors affect the seasonality of lamb – its breed and where it comes from. Technically speaking, lamb is any sheep that has not over-wintered, once it has it should be known as hogget, but this nicety is dying out. It's possible to eat lamb all year round, as the traditional, primitive breeds are born later in the year, are slower to mature, and are only ready for the table in January or February. Over the years, British lamb has become leaner but for the best flavour always choose it with a layer of clean, whitish fat. The colour of the meat can range from pearly pink to a deeper red as the season progresses. The texture, however, should be fine-grained, with a good, sharp finish and, for optimum flavour, lamb should be hung for a minimum of five days.

tip **Mutton chops in ale was an innkeeper's feast 200 years ago. If it's hung properly, mutton can be fried or roasted like lamb. Our mutton is very dense, like venison, and gamey in flavour.** Andrew Sharp, Herdwick Lamb

POULTRY

When buying chicken remember, you get what you pay for. A quality bird, free-ranging and slow-growing, with plenty of room to move about in, and fed on a good diet, will cost but will taste. When buying hen's eggs from the producer, it is the breed, diet they are fed and the freshness of the eggs that will affect their flavour. My favourite are Aracuna eggs I have gathered direct from the henhouse when staying with friends in Somerset, with their creamy, earthy yolk.

Poached Chicken Breast with Summer Vegetables

Serves four

Combine free-range chicken breasts with delicate summer vegetables to produce a light, fresh and colourful dish. If you can, use home-made chicken stock.

1 bunch of asparagus
4 baby courgettes
50gm / 2oz baby spinach leaves
600ml / 20 floz fresh chicken stock
4 free-range skinned chicken
    breasts 190gm / 7.5oz
zest of half a lemon
75gm / 3oz podded and peeled broad
    beans
1 bunch of spring onions, trimmed
    and cut in half lengthways
12gm / ½ oz picked chervil leaves
12gm / ½oz snipped chives
salt and white milled pepper

1 Prepare the asparagus by snapping the bottom quarter off and cutting the spear in half, on the angle. Cut the courgettes into three across their body, on the angle. Wash the spinach.

2 Place the chicken stock in a pan with the chicken breasts and bring to the boil. Reduce the heat and simmer for 5 minutes. Add the asparagus and lemon zest, then in 3 minute intervals add the broad beans, spring onions, and finally the courgettes. Simmer for a further 3 minutes.

3 Lift the breasts with the vegetables out of the pan and keep warm.

4 Turn up the heat and reduce the cooking liquor by three-quarters to intensify its flavour.

5 Turn down the heat, add the spinach leaves and simmer for a minute or until wilted. Check the seasoning, add the herbs and pour over the chicken and vegetables.

NEWLA EGG

tip My family were farmers in Punjab, India. We raised chickens and would make a chicken pickle – the recipe is around 500 years old. It's a real delicacy in India – it's made with chicken, garam masala, ginger, garlic, chilli and lime. Prabh Sandhu, Temptings

tip Our Label Anglais chicken is a free-range, traditional breed that takes a long time to mature. Cooking it produces a series of pleasing surprises: it smells wonderful; the skin roasts to a crisp, golden brown; the dark leg meat is particularly flavoursome, and the bones make a superb stock. Lee Mullet, Wyndham House Poultry

tip Venison has just under half the fat of chicken and half the cholesterol. It's probably the healthiest red meat you can eat. Peter Kent, West Country Venison

GAME

Game is classified into two types: furred, such as venison, rabbit and hare; and feathered, such as grouse, pheasant and wild duck. Most game, with the exception of rabbit, hare and pigeon, is protected by law and can only be shot or culled between certain dates, the rest of the year being closed season. All game birds should be hung, for how long depends on your taste, and how high you like the meat. So when buying, always ask how long it has already been hung. Older specimens should be stewed and casseroled, whereas young are best roasted.

Britain is particularly rich for game birds, as well as pheasant and partridge there are wild ducks, such as mallard, teal and widgeon, and snipe and woodcock. With their relatively low fat content, both furred and feathered game make healthy alternatives to farmed meat. The disadvantage is that they have to be cooked carefully to prevent the flesh from drying out.

FISH & SHELLFISH

When setting out to buy fresh fish whether freshwater, sea or shellfish the same fundamental rules always apply; if it's fresh it should glisten with a translucent shine, its eyes should gleam, the gills should be filled with bright red oxygenated blood, it should smell of airy sea breezes and still be pert or, to use the technical term, stiff alive.

Marinated Smoked Haddock

Serves four to six

A favourite recipe of Henrietta Green, who has been quick-marinating smoked haddock for years, whenever she needs a quick but impressive first course. Her recommendation is to "choose undyed, cold-smoked haddock – nothing but the finest, freshest will do. Ask for a piece cut from a large fillet and, if possible, its top end that tends to be fatter and juicier than the tail".

500g/1lb 2oz smoked haddock
zest and juice of 1 lemon
4 tbsp extra virgin olive oil
3 spring onions, finely chopped
(including green tops)
bunch of flat leaf parsley, finely
chopped
freshly ground black pepper

1 Remove the skin and bone from the piece of smoked haddock. With a very sharp knife, cut it at a slant into tissue-paper thin slices and arrange them on a plate so they are just overlapping. (You may find it easier to cut if you chill the fillet of haddock first – about 30 minutes in the freezer should do the trick.)

2 Mix the lemon juice and olive oil and then dribble about two-thirds over the fish. Scatter over the spring onions and parsley, pour over the remainder of the olive oil mixture and season with pepper.

3 Leave to stand for at least 15 minutes, longer if in the fridge. Serve with wodges of wholemeal or rye bread.

MARK HIX IN MY BASKET

Chef director of Caprice Holdings, Mark is also the chef at London's restaurant, The Ivy.

How often do you go to Borough?
I normally go down on a Friday morning.

What do you buy?
You never know what you are going to stumble across. I love it when Tony Booth has just a kilo of something special, like chicken-of-the-woods or proper, wiry wild asparagus from Spain – that always goes into the bag.

What's your favourite product?
I love the really rare stuff that you never see on restaurant menus that you can serve at home and surprise everyone with.

What is most significant about the re-emergence of markets like Borough?
It's about small producers and suppliers showing their wares to the general public and to the business. Sometimes these producers just don't get out there on the mainstream supplier circuit and are unknown. I do, though, find it frustrating, but take my hat off to suppliers like Furness Fish, who just don't supply restaurants. They have such a variety of fish and unusual shellfish like gooseneck barnacles and squat lobsters. I suppose if they did start supplying they would be like any old fishmonger – or would they?

Has Borough introduced you to ingredients you hadn't come across before?
Always. It's an eye opener and I encourage my chefs to go on a weekly basis. It makes you a better and more creative person.

Do you take your kids to the market?
No, they live in Manchester, or I would take them every week to encourage them to eat properly and see the raw products.

Did you go to food markets as a child?
I lived in Dorset and my grandfather used to grow vegetables, especially great tasting tomatoes, and I used to fish, so it was all on my doorstep.

When did you first discover the market?
Probably as soon as it re-emerged as a market for the general public to use.

Do you have a ritual when you go?
I love going down to Borough when I'm doing a dinner party at home with no pre-conceived ideas about what I'm going to cook. That idea scares most people, but cooking is mainly about ingredients and a shopping list can normally disappoint.

tip **The best way to eat smoked eel is the simplest: with a squeeze of lemon and some black pepper. It's a very oily fish, so it needs the lemon to cut through this. The Swedish eat eel for breakfast with scrambled eggs and parsley, served on top of rye bread.** Michael Brown, Brown & Forrest

FRESHWATER FISH
Considering the number of rivers flowing through Britain and the thousands of anglers patiently spending hour after hour on the banks with rod, line, or net in hand, it's surprising how few freshwater fish we actually eat. Salmon, trout and eel are all well-known, but there are several other, less well-known species which are worth seeking out; these include Char, which is a speciality of Lake Windemere, Carp, Perch, Tench, Bream, Pike and Zander. Freshwater fish are best if caught from clear, clean rivers. When they come from the brackish waters of slow-running rivers or deep stagnant ponds, there is a danger of their tasting a little dank and muddy.

SEAFISH
Critically, there are three types of seafish:

Oily, in which the oil is dispersed throughout the flesh, such as anchovy, herring, mackerel, sardine, sprat and tuna.

White fish, which can be round or flat. The most common is cod. Most of that which is on sale is deep-sea cod, caught in trawl-nets of boats which spend several weeks at sea. They obviously have to preserve their haul so they clean, gut and freeze the fish while still at sea. It's a pity, really. Fishermen tell me that aboard ship they prefer to eat it rested, or a day old, when its succulent, meaty flesh has firmed up and its sweetness has intensified – we should be so lucky! Occasionally you will see inshore cod and codling (baby cod) for sale and these may have landed on the slab unfrozen. Buy them if they look fresh. Other members of the extensive cod family include haddock, hake, ling, whiting and coley. Other favourites among round fish include sea bass, John Dory, monk fish and red mullet.

Flat fish should be treated with care, as they break up easily, and are generally best cooked simply, for example by grilling, poaching or dipping them in flour and pan frying them in butter, such as Dover sole and lemon sole; halibut, plaice and witch, also known as Torbay sole, are all more coarsely textured and flavoured and may be steamed, fried or stuffed and baked.

tip Black cod (picture, near right) has nothing to do with cod – it's not part of the cod family as some might think. It's actually part of the sable species, a category of fish with delicate textures and buttery flavours. **Delicious!** Graham Applebee, Applebee's Fish

Market thoughts

Mike Hobbs
Owner of Hobbs' Barber Shop, former market porter.

I started working in Borough when I was 18. I grew up in Dulwich and came to the market a lot as a kid. I'm now 39. I used to be 'on the stones'. That meant you were a casual market porter – you'd hang around the market – on the stones – waiting for someone to ask you for a helping hand and they'd pay you a few bob. I worked from 2am until 12noon. There weren't many young people working in the market. In fact, most of the stallholders were in their 60s then.

The old porters would fight like you wouldn't believe. One time a guy bit someone's ear off – like Mike Tyson. The porters earned good money. But they were drinking it as quickly as they were making it.

I worked for a guy called 'Old Harry'. He was 72 then – he's obviously not alive now. He hired me as an all around guy – I was the clerk, porter, I did whatever needed to be done. I grew up very quickly. Working for so many old people, I was surrounded by a lot of wisdom. It's hard now, because a lot of these people are getting on.

I had no idea what I was going to do. When the market started to decline I was in my 20s. All these old guys could go off and retire. I went to the barber to get my hair cut and thought 'I can do that'. I looked in the library and found a three-month course. After three months, there was no way I was ready to cut someone's hair. But I had no choice.

I made my first barbershop out of a trailer. It was 14ft long and 7ft wide. The chairman of the market gave me permission to put it in the car park. I called it 'Something for the weekend, Sir?' The porters called me Teasy-Weasy – he was a well-known hairdresser who pre-dates the likes of Vidal Sassoon. He was the first fashionable hairdresser.

I had a plastic sink and a kettle – that's how I washed people's hair. Before my first customer arrived, I burnt the kettle out so I had to borrow some hot water from the building where the restaurant 'Fish!' is now. All I had to put it in was a green watering-can. My wife Julie runs the pie shop – Hobbs' Pie Shop, directly across the road from where my barbershop is now.

I feel like I belong in Borough. It's as if I've sprung up from the ground here – my roots are deeply planted in and around this market so much so that I feel I couldn't escape, even if I wanted to. And I have a responsibility to preserve its history. A woman named Judy Richardson who worked in the market long ago, gave me all of her large black and white and sepia photos. So I have to ensure the memories of the old market linger on.

There are times when I love this place, others when I absolutely hate it. I haven't left the market so on one hand I probably know it better than most, on the other, I haven't seen the rest of the world.

Hake with Peas and Parsley

Serves four

An adaption from a Jane Grigson recipe, cook this in late spring as the delicate flavours and fresh colours herald the start of summer.

4 x 150gm / 6oz hake steaks
175gm / 7oz fresh podded peas
3 large cloves of garlic
100ml / 4floz fish stock
1 glass dry white wine
2 tbsps fresh chopped parsley
salt, lemon juice, plain flour, olive oil

1 Season the hake with salt and lemon juice and leave for at least an hour. Before cooking, drain, dry and turn in the flour.

2 In a large pot, heat enough olive oil to cover the base comfortably and cook the garlic until golden brown. Remove the garlic and put in the hake, adding the stock and wine. Bring to the boil.

3 Add peas and 2 tbsps of parsley; reduce the heat to allow the liquid to simmer gently. Cook for approximately 4-5 minutes, depending on the thickness of the fish. If you like, you can crush the garlic into a paste and add to the pot, otherwise discard it. As the fish cooks turn it once. Shake the pot so a sauce forms.

4 Check the fish by inserting a knife into it. It is cooked when the flesh starts to separate. Add more fresh parsley and serve.

SHELLFISH

The British coast is rich in shellfish, much of which is exported to France. Lobsters from the clear cold waters of the Minch off the Scottish coast are amongst the best in the world. Look out also for crawfish with its firm, creamy white meat. There are numerous shrimp, both brown and pink, and prawns swimming around our shores. Apart from the Dublin Bay Prawn, no large prawns inhabit our cold, northern seas. We do, however, have Cornish or Cromer brown crabs which are full of buttery richness and are at their best in summer, and scallops and mussels which are meatier and with fuller flavours during winter. We have two types of oysters, first the round, crinkly shelled native oyster that can be eaten when there is an 'r' in the month. These are sold under British natives – Colchester, Whitstable, Helford and so on. It is, in fact, perfectly safe to eat them all year round, but during the summer months they are spawning and more milky. Then, throughout Britain but particularly in Scotland, one finds Pacific oysters, farmed throughout the year – and also Portuguese oysters. They tend to be longer and thinner and are thought to be less delicate in flavour. The reason you can eat these through the seasons is because they are used to warmer waters so they don't spawn in the summer months, but you will sometimes find them a little milky in the hotter months because they are almost on the turn.

There are so many British shellfish to choose from, try to be brave, take the market fishmongers' advice and try new things.

Potted Shrimps

Serves four

Brown shrimps are one of our great shellfish delicacies, and they made the bay at Morecambe famous. Combined with this aromatic butter, their flavour is enhanced and preserved a little longer. Buy them ready peeled from the market to avoid having to do it yourself.

1 small shallot, finely chopped
280gm / 10oz unsalted butter
1 tsp anchovy essence
325gm / 12oz peeled brown shrimps
1 small bunch of dill, chopped
ground white pepper

1 Over a low heat sweat the shallot in 25gm / 1oz of the butter until translucent. Then add the remainder of the butter and leave to melt. Remove the pan from the heat and leave to cool slightly.

2 Stir the anchovy essence, dill, shrimps and a pinch of pepper into the melted butter. Spoon the mixture into four ramekins, pressing down firmly, place into the fridge and leave to set.

3 Serve with dressed salad leaves, wedges of lemon and wholemeal or granary toast. Once potted, the shrimps should keep for 3 days.

tip By law, you can only sell native 'flat' oysters between May 14 and August 4. Their flesh is more delicate than rock oysters. People think they should only eat oysters if there's an 'r' in the month. But rock oysters are perfectly safe, and tasty, to eat all year round. *Richard Haward, Richard Haward Oysters*

DELI & STORE

Borough Market isn't just a bounty of fresh meat, fish, fruit and vegetables. The market also does a roaring trade in the best quality delicatessan products available from around the country – and across the world. Take your pick from the wide range of delicacies dried, tinned, bottled, potted, smoked or preserved. It's a true gourmand's dream.

ROSE GRAY IN MY BASKET

Co-founder of the River Café, Rose fell in love with markets when she was living in Florence – the home of her in-laws. "The River Café's food was inspired by my mother-in-law, Dada, who was a stickler for simplicity. As she lay dying, she called her to her bedside and whispered: 'Go easy on the herbs, not so many herbs.'"

How often do you go to Borough?
I've been going to Borough Market from the start – when it first opened to the public. I go every two weeks. But my husband, the artist, David MacIlwaine, goes every week.

What do you buy?
I have to have salted anchovies from Brindisa and their capers. They also do really good sun-dried tomatoes. I also adore the Italian Piedmontese cheese from Gastronomica. The fish stalls are great for kippers and other native fish.

What's your favourite product? What do you do with it?
The salted anchovies are my favourite. I use them to make an anchovy and rosemary sauce.

What do you think is most significant about the re-emergence of markets like Borough?
It gives the smaller producers a chance to find a market.

How would you compare Borough Market to other great markets in the world?
Borough Market hasn't quite reached the same scale as the world's great markets. But the smaller stalls offer good seasonal vegetables and the crème fraîche and Stilton from Neal's Yard are delicious. Give it time and Borough could compete.

If you could have your own stall at Borough what would you sell?
I'd sell a wide selection of extra virgin olive oil from different single Italian estates – from the spicy to the more mellow.

From Scandic highlights like pickled herring and gravadlax to handmade Swiss muesli or prepared seaweed from Ireland, the market more than competes with the finest department store foodhalls for its superb range of prepared foods and key ingredients from across Europe – and further afield. Look out for every kind of olive oil, from the simplest virgin for daily cooking, to those reserves as revered as the finest wines. In the tinned category, anchovies from Spain and goose fat and foie gras from southwest France are market bests. If looking for cured meats, the choice of Italian hams and Spanish chorizo are hard to beat. And then there are the olives, a true cornucopia of types and flavours to suit every taste. And, of course, there are the pickles and chutneys, too, simply made to accompany many of the market's meats and cheeses.

tip Ortiz anchovies are fished just off the Basque region of northern Spain. They're not hairy because each anchovy is trimmed and filleted by hand. They're also a lot larger than most because the anchovies are hand selected. The rule is: the bigger the tin, the bigger the fish is inside. Alistair Cameron, Brindisa Spanish Foods

tip There is good and bad tofu. Most people have only experienced the latter – it's the equivalent of sliced white: i.e. mass-produced and heavily pasteurised to extend the shelf-life. Good quality fresh tofu should have a creamy smooth texture and no sour aftertaste.

Neil McClennan, Clean Bean

Salad of Wood Pigeon, Wild Boar Pancetta and Mixed Leaves

Serves four

Sold in a large piece, for all its fancy name pancetta is in fact bacon. With its earthy flavour, wild boar pancetta from Sillfield Farm goes really well with pigeon.

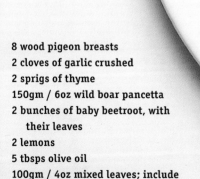

8 wood pigeon breasts
2 cloves of garlic crushed
2 sprigs of thyme
150gm / 6oz wild boar pancetta
2 bunches of baby beetroot, with
    their leaves
2 lemons
5 tbsps olive oil
100gm / 4oz mixed leaves; include
    curly endive and rocket
salt and freshly ground black pepper

1 Pre-heat the oven to 200C / 400F / gas 6.

2 Remove the beetroot leaves from the beets, wash them and mix with the washed salad leaves. Trim the stems back to within an inch of the beets, put them into a roasting tray with 2 tbsps of olive oil, one clove of garlic and season. Put into the oven, roasting for 35-40 minutes until tender. Allow to cool slightly, then rub the skins off on a dry cloth. Quarter and return to the oil in the roasting pan adding the remainder of the olive oil and the juice of the lemons. Add more seasoning, if needed, and set aside.

3 Cut the pancetta into slices, then across, to make short sticks. Fry them off in a frying pan gently to start, then increase the heat allowing them to cook in their own fat until they become crispy. Remove from the pan, reserving the fat in the pan.

4 Season the pigeon breasts and fry off for 2 minutes on each side with the garlic and thyme, making sure they are well-coloured. Remove from pan and rest for 5 minutes, keeping warm. Drain off the fat then deglaze with 2 tbsps of water, scraping the residue from the base of the pan until nearly dry. Add the beetroot and dressing, allowing it to warm slightly.

5 To serve, toss the salad leaves, pancetta and beetroot in half of the dressing. Cut the wood pigeon in half through the breasts, place on top and dress with the remainder.

jules & sharpie's
hot mint jelly

Ingredients: sugar, **mint 5%**, cider vinegar, apple pectin, **hot peppers 2%**

Refrigerate after opening

Warning: this product **contains hot peppers** and must be **used with caution**
350g

tip **People are used to bresaola made with beef, but in Sardinia we cure tuna in the same way – with fresh air and Italian sea salt. It keeps for months and is magnificent with a bit of lemon, pepper, a drizzle of extra virgin olive oil and rocket.** Enrico Chessa, Villanova

tip **The best way to bring out the flavours of a good single-estate coffee is to filter it. The last thing I would do is put it through an espresso machine. The sheer pressure doesn't bring out the coffee's best qualities.** Anita le Roy, Monmouth Coffee Company

me: LE CHIANCHE (D.O.P.)
gin: Puglia (Italy)
e of olives: Ogliarola +
Leccino
idity: 0.35%
ssing: First Cold Press
cription: Robust & intense with
assy & peppery aftertaste
gestion: Best served raw in
ps or on grilled meat or
ed vegetables.

250ml   500ml   1000ml
£3.40 £6.00 £9.50

NAME: OLEARIA CAPOLEUCA
Origin: Puglia (Italy)
Type of olives: Cellina di Nardò,
Ogliarda & Leccino
Acidity: 0.5%
Pressing: First Cold Press
Description: A medium fruity
oil with a nutty & peppery aftertaste
Suggestion: Perfect for your every
day use; either for cooking or as a
compliment to any dish.

250ml   500ml   1000ml
£2.50 £4.75 £6.90

NAME: Labbate IL Vergin
Origin: Puglia (Italy)
Type of olives: Cellina + Leccino
Acidity: 1.5%
Description: A medium fruity
virgin olive oil with a finishi
almond fragrance.
Suggestion: A perfect virgin o
to be used for your cooking. I
enhance the flavour of your
dishes.

1000ml £5.40

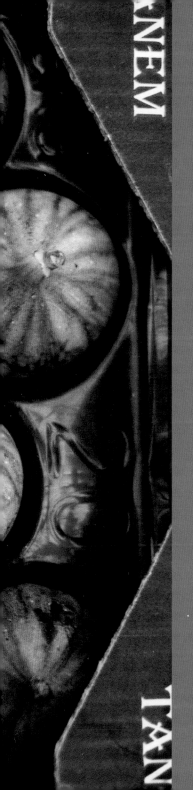

FRUIT 'N VEG

Despite the temptation presented to us all by the glorious array of imported fruit and vegetables on sale throughout the year, as a general principal I prefer to buy fresh home-grown fruit and vegetables in season. Not only does it make sense financially, as they are often cheaper, but, more importantly, it is when they are at their best.

VEGETABLES are categorised by the part of the plant we eat. At Borough you should be able to find all sorts of delicacies, so keep a look out for them and remember, one of the joys of shopping at a market is to be bold, to experiment and to discover new tastes and flavours – ask when you don't know what something is, it is bound to be good!

Roots & Tubers Most root vegetables are in season during the winter, and are well-suited to soups, stews, gratins and braises. Some of the most unattractive looking roots mask delicacies lying just beneath their surfaces. Look out for spring or young white turnips, which are far smaller and sweeter than their larger winter or maincrop varieties. Steam their leafy tops, toss them in olive oil, slightly sharpened with lemon juice, and serve them as a salad. The young leaves of scorzonera and salsify, also known as vegetable oyster, can be enjoyed in salads in the same way.

Another ugly delicacy is celeriac. Don't be put off by the scabby appearance of the root, as underneath its pock-marked skin lies a treasure trove of nutty juiciness – but avoid the large knobs as they can be woody and or even woolly in texture. Horseradish is an equally misshapen root and is not easy to come by, when you see it fresh, snap it up. If you peel and grate it and put it in a jar with a little wine vinegar it will keep for ages in the fridge.

Brassicas This group includes a wide range of vegetables, some of the cultivated varieties such as the cauliflower and broccoli, were known to have been eaten by the Ancient Greeks and Romans and cabbage was certainly grown by the Saxons and Celts. So they must number amongst the green vegetables with the longest culinary tradition. Look out for Savoy cabbages, with a milder flavour than the smooth-leaved winter cabbage, it can be shredded raw for salads and makes a welcome change to the ubiquitous coleslaw made with the crispy but dull Dutch white cabbage. I am also keen on the nutty kale and curly kale, whose leaves should be firm, free of blemishes and have a good, clear, even colour.

Stalks, stems and leaves Cardoons, rarely seen in the shops, are one of the most underrated of vegetables. A member of the thistle family, and closely related to the globe artichoke, it is the stalk rather than the flower heads or choke which is eaten. The stalks are cut when still young and tender, lightly blanched and eaten like celery in soups, salads and stews. Seskale, another rare delicacy, is in season only briefly in early spring. The baby leaf stalks are grown under cloches or earth banks, to emerge pallid and frail. They should be lightly boiled or steamed and eaten with a hollandaise sauce.

Later in April come hop shoots or 'bines', which are thinned from the hop plants. These must be cut before they grow thick and hairy and are cooked simply in the same way as seakale. Both these young shoots taste like asparagus and I always think of them as overtures to the main work.

Asparagus has a short season in Britain, lasting only from May to late June. The best shoots or spears are firm and taught, fleshy with not a hint of woodiness, and with the tips still tightly closed. Other vegetables in this family include celery, both white and green, Florence or bulb fennel, with its slight aniseed taste, spinach, spinach beet and chard.

Salad vegetables When thinking salad most people start with lettuce. Thankfully, the range of salad leaves available has increased dramatically over the past few years. Look out for chicory, raddicchio, endives, lamb's lettuce, rocket, watercress, winter cress and purslane to add range of flavour, texture and colours.

Potatoes Coming from the same tuber family as Deadly Nightshade, what we eat are the tubers which form on the plant's underground stems. These are vital for the plant's survival and reproduction, as it is there that it stores carbohydrates and water. The colour of the skin can vary from a pale, thin cream through a rosy pink to a dark, conker-brown, and the flesh anything from milky white to deep yellow. British potatoes fall into three categories.

'Earlies' from the beginning of June, herald the start of summer and are firm and waxy with a strong earthy taste. When they are first lifted they have a very high dry-matter content making them perfect for boiling. As they mature, the starch content rises and the waxy texture disappears; they become softer as they cook and their skin thickens. To make sure you are buying a true early, rub its skin with your finger: it should flake off readily as it has, to use the technical jargon, no 'skin set'. The most common British varieties are Home Guard, Arran Comet, Ulster Sceptre, Pentland Javelin and Maris Bard.

'Second Earlies' are on sale from July-September and include the Wilkar, which is particularly good for sauteeing, and the Estima, an adequate all-rounder.

'Maincrop' potatoes are ready to be harvested from September onwards. The best-known is the red-skinned Desiree, with its high dry-matter content and light yellow flesh, which is ideal for boiling and makes reasonably good chips; Maris Piper for excellent chips, Pentland Squire with its texture well-suited for mashing, Cara, recognisable by its spotted pink skin, ideal for baking, and King Edward, known as Kerr's Pink in Scotland, which roasts well and makes good chips.

Whether each variety has its own inherent flavour is a matter of some controversy as so many factors affect flavour – such as soil, climate, weather patterns, farming practices and the degree of maturity. Always make sure the potato you buy is appropriate for the method of cooking, that it is fresh and firm, with unbroken skin (except for earlies) and never buy any with green areas or sprouting roots. It means that they have been left lying around in the light too long and are becoming toxic.

Fruiting vegetables Forming a loose collection, what these vegetables have in common is that we eat the fruit containing the seeds. If the fruit is under-ripe, it will be too firm and lacking any inherent flavour; but if it is over-ripe the seeds or pips will be too large and tough and the flesh pappy. Examples include vegetable marrows, courgettes, pumpkins and squashes. Look out particularly for the summer squash or patty pan, which, when small and young may be cooked in their skin.

tip Smoked garlic gets sweeter, tasting more like a chestnut than garlic. Some people eat it on its own. My favourite recipe is placing a bulb cut into two halves in the cavity of a chicken. The oak smoke and mild garlic flavours come through the chicken.

Colin Boswell, The Garlic Farm on the Isle of Wight

Roasted Autumn Vegetables

Serves four

In autumn Borough Market is ablaze with knobbly-shaped gourds and squashes. This recipe uses two varieties, but choose any others you prefer. Always go for squashes that are firm skinned and unblemished.

1 acorn squash cut into rough 5cm / 2 inch chunks

1 butternut squash [approx. 750gm / 1.9 lb] peeled and cut into 5cm / 2 inch chunks

4 red onions peeled and cut into wedges of six

2 medium heads of fennel cut into quarter wedges

6 small red skinned potatoes, cut in half

6 sprigs of thyme

75ml / 3floz olive oil

salt and freshly ground black pepper

1 Preheat the oven to 220C /425F / gas 7. Toss all the prepared vegetables in a roasting tray with the olive oil, thyme and plenty of seasoning.

2 Roast for about 45 minutes, taking them out and tossing and turning them at 15 minute intervals.

3 The vegetables are cooked when they are tender, slightly charred and have caramelised in their own natural sugars.

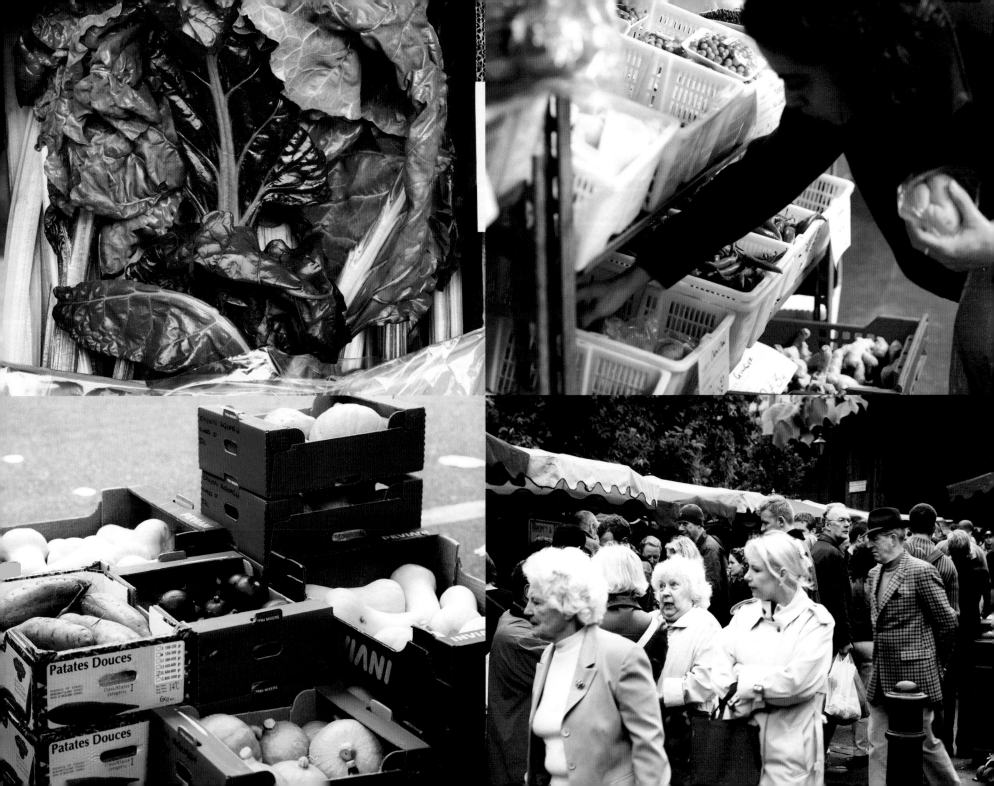

FRUIT

It has always struck me as curious that, although the supermarket shelves are filled all year round with mangoes, pineapples, bananas, mangosteens, pomegranates, kumquats, rambutans and just about any other exotic fruit you care to mention, you cannot buy much in the way of varieties of our home-grown top fruit from trees, and soft fruit from bushes.

Obviously it would be ridiculous to restrict ourselves to home-grown fruit, for example, it would mean ignoring the treasures of the citrus fruits, as we just cannot grow them in our climate. Nevertheless, at Borough expect to see our own quality home-grown fruit available in season.

Fruit from the trees During the summer and early autumn the orchards are heavy with fruit. First come the cherries, then hot on their heels come the cooking plums, swiftly followed by eating plums, like the orangey-red Victorias, the purplish-black Kirk's Blues, and the pale, sugary greengages. The other members of the plum family such as damsons, bullaces and sloes will not ripen until early autumn, when they are ready for bottling, turning into jams and jellies or using for

flavouring gin – a traditional Christmas day favourite.

Apple lovers from all over the world agree that Britain produces the finest apples, as for once, our climate works to our advantage. Ideal conditions for apples are plenty of rain to swell the fruit, comparatively low temperatures for slow ripening, weak sun to colour the fruit and cool nights to intensify the flavour; this pretty much sums up British summer!

Some apples are ripe for eating by mid-August, as are some pears; but you will have to wait until October to enjoy home-grown quinces. The hardier Medlar will not be ready until early October, when it is picked from the branch, 'bletted', ie soft, brown and half-rotten.

In Brogdale in Kent, home of the British National Fruit Collection, there are over 3,000 named varieties of apple. No two apple varieties are ever alike, and no other fruit has such a wide range of tastes, aromas, textures, colours and shapes. Unfortunately, we are in danger of losing some of the old-fashioned and less well-known apples that are grown on too small a scale to satisfy the quantities which the

Summer Fruit Soup with Thick Cream

Serves four

This vibrant dish can be prepared
well ahead of time, using any berries
available, and it makes a refreshing
change to have soup at the
end of the meal.

SYRUP
450ml / 18floz water
1 glass rosé wine
150gm / 6oz caster sugar
1 cinnamon stick
1 tsp orange zest
1 sprig of mint

FRUIT
75gm / 3oz raspberries
50gm / 2oz redcurrants
50gm / 2oz blueberries
50gm / 2oz blackcurrants
75gm / 3oz strawberries, hulled
4 large mint leaves
150ml / 6floz double cream, lightly whipped

1 Make the syrup by
   dissolving the sugar in the
   water over a low heat. Add
   the cinnamon, orange zest
   and wine, turn up the heat
   and simmer for 3 minutes.
2 Remove from the heat and
   add the mint. Put in the
   fridge and leave to chill.
3 To serve, mix the fruit
   together and divide evenly
   between four soup bowls.
   Pour over the syrup, add a
   dollop of thick double
   cream, tear the mint
   leaves into small pieces
   and scatter over the top.

supermarkets demand. Have you ever eaten Worcester Pearmain, with its dense, strawberry taste, the tiny Pitmaston Pine Apple, with its hint of pineapple, or Lady Sudeley, which has been grown for well over 150 years? There are also the creamy Ribston Pippi, Tyderman's Late Orange, and Ashmead's Kernel, which reminds you of acid drops. These are just a few of my favourites.

Like apples there are several varieties of pear and each one has a distinctive flavour and a natural season. The best known is the Conference. Sharp and firm, it is slightly gritty in texture and easily distinguished by its long, tapered shape and heavily-russeted green skin; it is a good all-rounder and may be cooked or eaten raw. The Doyenne de Comice is fatter, more conically shaped and far sweeter, as is the Williams Bon Chretien, which is pale yellow, sometimes flushed with red, and has a particularly soft, yielding flesh. Real connoisseurs favour the Beurre Hardy, which as its name suggests, melts like butter in the mouth.

Fruit from the bushes Late June to September is the season for soft fruit. There is a profusion of blackcurrants, redcurrants and white currants; tiny irridescent cooking gooseberries, and the full blown 'levellers', or 'eaters' such as strawberries in all their juicy glory, the softer and subtler raspberry and the larger, darker loganberry with its sharper taste. Finally comes the blackberry which may be picked from hedgerows right up to mid-October, although according to an old country superstition blackberries should never be touched after Michaelmas day, October 10, as on this day the Devil is said to spit on the fruit to spite his rival, the Archangel Michael.

tip **Blueberries are the healthiest of all berries. They have more antioxidants than any other fruit or vegetable. They reduce cholesterol, they're very good for blood flow, they help your eyesight and they taste good. The only bad thing is they're only in season from July to August.** David Trehane, Dorset Blueberry

HERBS
Herbs are essential in cooking for their taste, smell and colour. Every keen cook should have a herb garden, or at very least, a sunny window ledge packed with pots. When cutting or plucking sprigs, or leaves from a herb plant, try to use either tips, side shoots or lateral leaves to encourage new growth. Always buy cut herbs when they look perky, and avoid any which show signs of wilting or if the leaves are changing colour.

There are quite a few superb combinations of foods and herbs to keep as a mental checklist when visiting the market, which complement and balance each other's flavours; eggs with sorrel; chicken with tarragon, lamb with rosemary, peas with mint, tomatoes with basil, broad beans with summer savory, rhubarb with sweet cicely (to avoid some of the tartness), dill with salmon and mackerel with fennel.

Nevertheless, I am all in favour of cooks experimenting for themselves, as this is the only way that their repertoire of herbs can be broadened. With few exceptions, however, I do insist on using flat leaf rather than moss-curled, or curly leaf parsley. I know the moss-curled variety is grown all year-round and is very British, but I just do not like its grainy, coarse texture and its overwhelming flavour. Flat leaf parsley is far softer and subtler and enhances the flavour of the food rather than overwhelming it.

ANTONIO CARLUCCIO IN MY BASKET

A mushroom obsessive lover of good food, Antonio owns Carluccio's, the popular chain of Italian cafés, as well as the Neal Street restaurant in London's Covent Garden.

What do you buy at the market?
I tend to buy unusual fruits or vegetables and eat them on their own so I can better understand their flavours. I go there to be inspired, to speak to stall holders and for entertainment.

Is there a stall you always visit?
I could speak with Tony from The Mushroom Company for hours – I always pay a visit to him. I love to see Marco Fiore from Gastronomica, as well.

If you could have your own stall at Borough Market, what would you sell?
I am a man obsessed with mushrooms! Need you ask?

How often do you go to Borough?
Once a month.

What three adjectives best describe Borough Market?
Seasonal, fresh, ethnic.

What do you think is most significant about the re-emergence of markets like Borough?
It's finally a breath of fresh air for this country.

How would you compare Borough Market to other great markets in the world?
Embryonic.

Did you go to food markets as a child?
Yes, to the major markets in Turin, Venice and Florence, which were full of local surprises.

Do you have a ritual when you go to Borough?
I always buy a bacon roll from Sillfield.

With which literary or historic character would you compare Borough Market?
Dionysus

FUNGHI

At Borough look out for porcini, the most treasured of all Italian mushrooms, known in France as cep and England as penny bun. They are in season from early summer through to the autumn, have a dense, meaty flavour and are strangely slippery, almost gelatinous in texture. Their flavour is second to none. Dried, they are sold throughout the year and add body and depth of flavour to stews, casseroles and sauces.

In Britain the season starts with the St George's mushroom, traditionally found in grassy hedgerows, wood edges and pastures on and around April 23, St George's Day. The season progresses with the pitted morel, then come dusky orange chantarelles.

Later in the year arrive meaty field mushrooms, soft, shaggy ink caps, giant puffballs, delicate wild oyster mushrooms, chicken-of-the-woods and field blewits, with their stalks brushed purple.

Truffles also find their way to market. These underground tubers are dug up by specially-trained dogs or pigs. The Italian white truffle is superb grated raw over a risotto; and the black truffle from France is used in pates and stuffings, or even baked in batter like miniature Yorkshire puddings.

tip Make sure that the black or white truffles you're buying are fresh. If they feel soft or have soft spots, they're starting to decay. A good, fresh specimen will even bounce if you drop it on the floor. Paul Wheeler, The Wild Mushroom Co.

BAKERY

One of the things you'll notice when visiting the Borough Market is how many bread stalls there are. It comes as a great relief, particularly if you've been raised on the vagaries of supermarket sliced white. The range is phenomenal, ranging from five-day sourdough to half-an-hour soda bread and an ever-evolving range in between.

The craft element in the preparation of quality bread is critical to its flavour. The loaf you buy will be affected by the flour used, the length of its fermentation, its mix with other ingredients, and the type of oven in which it is cooked. Traditionally, a proper sourdough would be made over a six-day process. So many breads are made within the hour, with hardly a rising and certainly no knocking-back. The old-fashioned craft techniques were really developed to make bread taste as good as it could. The intensity of the heat and the nature of the oven are also critical. Woodburning stoves provide a drier, more even heat, for example, and some would say, are more environmentally friendly.

When buying your daily bread at Borough, expect to find no additives, but it is wise to check the salt and fat content, particularly as recently there have been supermarket scares about the levels. At Borough not only can you taste it, you can find out the precise measure in each slice.

tip **We use only the finest flour made from wheat grown and milled in France. Most of the bread you buy in the UK is made with flour from the US or Canada. French wheat tastes better and the milling process in France tends to be longer and slower.** Paul Rhodes, Duponds Bakery

Gypsy Toast with Roasted Plums and Clotted Cream

Serves four

Give good, old-fashioned eggy bread a modern twist with the tangy sweetness of perfect plums and the smooth depth of Cornish cream.

4 slices of white bread, cut thinly
4 eggs
50ml / 2floz milk
1 tsp ground cinnamon
25ml / 1floz vegetable oil
75gm / 3oz unsalted butter
10 plums firm fleshed (Victoria, Opal, Marjory)
75gm/ 3oz Demerara sugar
25ml / 1floz Marsala wine
2 tsp icing sugar
1 small tub of clotted cream

1 Preheat the oven to 220C / 425F / gas 7.
2 Halve the plums and remove stones, place in a roasting tray, cut side up. Sprinkle with cinnamon, Marsala and put a small knob of butter into the cavity left by the stone. Dredge the tops with the Demerara and leave for 30 minutes to marinade. Place the plums into the oven and roast for 20-30 minutes until the tops are bubbling and glazed.
3 In a bowl, whisk the eggs with the milk, cinnamon and half the icing sugar. Soak the bread in the mixture until sodden. Melt the remaining butter with the oil at a medium heat and fry the bread until golden brown on both sides.
4 To serve, dust with icing sugar, spoon 5 plum halves on top with the buttery sweet plum juice and finish with a dollop of clotted cream.

JEREMY LEE
IN MY BASKET

The head chef at Terence Conran's Blue Print Café in Butler's Wharf, Jeremy is fascinated by Borough Market. He asks, "is there a better way to see food than when it is piled high, stall after stall, in a market dripping in history?"

Which stalls do you always visit?
I always go to L.Booth to get the attention of Tony – he has wonderful British produce as well as extraordinary vegetable and fruit stuffs from far-flung lands. And I will listen to anyone if there is a possibility of a truffle at the end of the conversation! He is a very dear man. I also like to see Ben and Owen at Neal's Yard Dairy – they generously hand over samples of lovely cheese that I then add

to my menu at the Blue Print Café. Brindisa are old friends and their beautiful Spanish produce remains unequalled. And I love the sausages and bacon from The Ginger Pig.

If you could have your own stall at Borough Market, what would you sell?
My stall would have a Scottish theme, offering Scottish raspberries, Dundee pies, rolled oat bannocks, Aberdeen rowies, Arbroath smokies, mealie puddings and Findon haddock.

What is most significant about the re-emergence of markets like Borough?
I find it inspiring to see the abundance of lovely produce piled up on tables and the higgledy-piggledy heaps of goods always thrill. One can go without a shopping list and come away with an entire lunch or dinner made up simply from what one saw.

How would you compare Borough Market to other great markets in the world?
It is nudging eccentric for a city the scale of London.

If you could compare Borough Market with a literary character, who would it be?
Hobson of Hobson's Choice say I.

DAIRY

Milk is one of the most complete foods available but it is also used as the basis of all dairy produce, whether the source animal be cow, ewe, goat – or even buffalo. It is perhaps the traditional British cheeses in particular that have gained renewed exposure through the efforts of small, regional producers at the Borough Market.

CHEESE

For me, one of the wonders of food production is the turning of milk into cheese and the sheer diversity of textures, flavours, shapes and colours available at Borough Market today is nothing short of a miracle. Nothing has such a strong influence on cheese as the milk from which it is made, the type of animal it comes from and whether it be skimmed or semi-skimmed, fresh, raw or pasteurised, left to mature overnight or longer.

First the milk must be prepared, so a starter rennet is added: the starter introduces bacteria essential for the milk to ripen and the rennet causes the milk to curdle so it separates out into curds and whey. The curds are what the cheese is made of, so the whey must be drained away. (Although a few cheeses, such as ricotta, are actually made from the whey.)

Then begin the processes specific to the actual making of the cheese. These can include cutting, milling or kneading the curds, 'cheddaring' them (a process specific to Cheddar by which they are turned and stacked), heating them slightly, ladling them into moulds, or leaving them to drain naturally, salting them or leaving them to soak in brine for a saltier flavour, injecting them with mould for a blue cheese, or pressing them for semi-hard or hard cheese.

Finally there comes the process of ripening. Some cheeses are eaten fresh, within a day or so of being made; others may be aged for as long as three years. Again, depending on the cheese, the atmosphere in which they are matured may be damp

or dry – in a cellar, cave, or drying room – the cheese may be turned daily or every two weeks or so to ensure that it ripens evenly. It may be pierced, so a mould may develop within it, washed or brushed for a rind finish or for a bloom of mould to develop on its exterior; or even wrapped in a cloth or sealed in wax or fat.

Throughout the world countless different cheeses are made. They may be loosely divided into the following categories:

Fresh milk or unripened soft cheeses, such as fromage frais, Ricotta, Petit Suisse, curd cheese, cottage cheese or cream cheese.

Soft rind-washed cheeses, which have rinds ranging in colour from pale beige to deep orange; such as Munster, Pont-l'Éveque and Livarot.
Veined or blue cheeses such as cows milk Stilton and ewe's milk Roquefort.

Hard or pressed cheeses, such as Cheddar, Edam and Parmesan.

Pressed and cooked cheeses, made by the same process as hard cheeses except that the milk is heated to a high temperature and 'cooked' during the cutting stage, resulting in a rubbery cheese, such as Gruyère or Emmental.

Brined cheese, such as Feta, which originates from Greece and is made with ewe's milk.

In this country there has recently been an incredible revival of small cheesemakers, producing interesting cheeses on the farm, using the farm's own milk to give them specific and distinctive flavours. Some, like Gorwydd Caerphilly are beautifully-made, handcrafted old-fashioned territorial cheeses, others such as Beenleigh Blue will beat any Roquefort.

tip **We don't sell anything under 12-16 months old, which is unusual now. By old-fashioned standards, it was the norm. The Cheshire cheese you'll find in supermarkets is probably only 4-6 months old. But age intensifies the flavour. It's out of this world in dauphinoise potatoes.**
John Bourne, H.S. Bourne traditional Cheshire cheese

SEAN DAVIES IN MY BASKET

The executive chef at Tate Modern. Sean has worked with one of France's most renowned chefs, Paul Bocose, and goes every week to source food for the museum's top floor restaurant.

What do you buy at the market?
I buy loads from Neal's Yard Dairy: their goat's curd is on the Tate restaurant menu, as well as Tymsboro goat's cheese and Durrus Irish cheese. I buy lomo Iberico (cured pork loin) and a selection of cured meats (salchichon Iberico and leon cooking chorizo picante) from Brindisa, plus black and white puddings, fig and almond cake and smoked paprika. I buy dry cured bacon from Northfield Farm. The Fresh Olive Oil Company marinade Manzanilla olives in smoked paprika, lemon and garlic especially for us. All the bread we serve in the restaurant – French sticks, sourdoughs, breads made with splet flour – comes from Duponds Bakery. Ninety per cent of the restaurant's fruit and vegetables is bought from Turnips.

How do you use the ingredients?
I top grilled violet aubergines (from Turnips), piquillo peppers (from Brindisa) on olive sourdough bread (Duponds) with goat's curd (Neal's Yard) and basil (Turnips). One of my favourite dishes is roasted mackerel (Applebee's Fish) with chorizo (Brindisa) hash and smoked paprika (Brindisa) aioli. And my baked roscoff onion (Turnips) with fresh ceps (L. Booth's) is to die for.

What's the most interesting thing you've bought at the market?
Sumac from Arabica – to sprinkle it over a salad of Feta, watermelon and tomato.

If you had your own stall, what would you sell on it?
Fruit and vegetables. It's the one area that needs promoting. We need to have better access to properly grown and sourced produce.

Did you go to markets as a child?
I grew up in a Shropshire market town, where going to the market was a twice-weekly ritual. All of our shopping was done there. I remember walking down rows and rows of trellis tables set up with local game that still had its feathers, baskets of eggs and homemade cheeses, cakes, pickles and jams.

Do you have a ritual when you visit?
Yes, I go with my wife Karen and our two young daughters. We get there early and have a bacon sandwich from the stall at Northfield Farm. Then we head straight for Monmouth Coffee for an Americano and a double latté. Then we visit Freddy Foster from Turnips to catch up with the gossip. The girls love it when Kevin bursts into an operatic tune. We have a mapped out circuit, starting at Green Market, swinging by Brindisa and on to Neal's Yard.

If Borough Market were a literary character, who would it be?
Author, Charles Dickens, of course! Especially at Christmas, with all the turkeys and game hanging up over the stalls, the railway arches with the cast iron and glass ceiling, sawdust on the floor and the characters on the Herdwick Lamb stall dressed in their Victorian outfits, slicing meat on their original hand-operated meat slicers.

Brown Bread and Honey Ice Cream
Serves four to six

An excellent way to use excess
brown bread – and this delicious
ice cream stores well in the
freezer, too.

**100gm / 4oz fresh brown
breadcrumbs**
75gm / 3oz Demerara sugar
1 tsp ground cinnamon
5 tbsps clear, runny honey
4 whole eggs + 4 egg yolks
200gm / 7oz icing sugar
400ml / 14floz double cream

1 Mix breadcrumbs, Demerara sugar
and cinnamon on a baking sheet.
Place them under a hot grill for
about 2-3 minutes, stirring
occasionally, until the sugar melts
and starts to turn golden. Leave to
cool and set.

2 Whisk eggs and yolks with the
icing sugar until doubled in
volume and pale yellow, then add
the honey.

3 Break up the breadcrumb caramel
into about the size of one penny
pieces, put them into a bowl and
whisk with double cream until it
forms soft peaks. Carefully fold in
the egg mixture, pour into an ice
cream machine and churn until
set. Keep in a freezer until
required.

4 If you don't have an ice cream
machine keep the breadcrumb
mixture separate. Then put the
remainder of the ingredients in a
container and into the freezer.
After an hour the mixture should
be setting and showing ice
crystals on the top. Remove and
stir in the breadcrumb caramel,
then put it back into the freezer.
Repeat the stirring procedure
three or four times.

tip The butter I sell comes from a small farm in a town called Deux-Sévres, near the Cognac region in France, where it's handmade daily. The butter's unique because they churn it immediately after the cows have been milked, resulting in a rich, creamy flavour. It's ideal for making pastry.

Alex Cheesman, Real France

BUTTER AND CREAM At Borough you'll find the full range of butter, from traditional sweet-cream farmhouse butter, whey butter and even, at Neal's Yard Dairy, clotted cream butter; and from France, the wonderful, ripened Échiré butter, which is made with soured and ripened cream. There is also a wide range of creams on sale, including a Jersey clotted cream from Devon with a nutty flavour and a full-rounded richness that transforms the dullest of puddings.

127

TOASTED CHEESE SANDWICH
WITH POILÂNE SOURDOUGH BREAD £3—
MONTGOMERYS CHEDDAR
ONIONS LEEKS & GARLIC

STAFFORDSHIRE Oatcake Wrap
WITH MONTGOMERYS CHEDDAR, ONIONS £ 2·50
LEEKS & GARLIC

RACLETTE

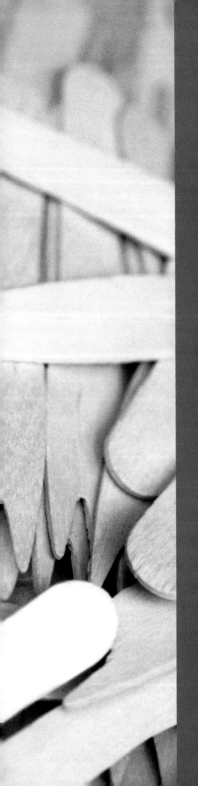

TREATS & SNACKS

The heart of Borough's retail market may lie in its fresh produce and delicacies, but perhaps its stomach lies in the ready-made food you can treat yourself to as you shop. A trip to Borough on a Friday or Saturday lunchtime will have your mouth watering as the scent of cooking bacon, melting cheese and warming roasts waft through the market.

It's not a bad idea to sample produce you might not previously have tried by buying a snack before making a fuller purchase – or maybe that's just an excuse for gluttony! From oysters to faggots, raclette cheese melted over fresh farmhouse bread, to the market's famous pork pies, there's a wide range of food produced for you to eat as you shop. But treats at Borough don't stop there. The finest chocolates and most delicious desserts are handmade to take away and serve back home. Traditional English puddings, French apple tarts and creamy yogurt pudding pots are all for sale. And don't forget to treat yourself to a bunch of the freshest cut flowers before making your way.

Market thoughts

You don't have to scoff a whole box of chocolates. Real, quality chocolate is so rich and so full of flavour that you're satisfied with a small amount. You can almost smell the cows from it. The cream I use for my chocolate is that fresh. It's really intense – from Normandy, France.

Gerard Coleman
Founder of L'Artisan du Chocolat.

I worked as a pastry chef with Jean Christophe Novelli. That's my background – I was a chef. I decided to set up on my own. I wanted to make chocolates for restaurants. Gordon Ramsay was one of my first clients. Then I opened a stall at Borough Market.

It was horrible at the start. There were only 14 or so stallholders. The market was held only twice a month. It was really cold in the winter. People were not coming that much, so we were all trying to keep ourselves entertained.

The market's a great arena for creativity. I get ideas from customers all the time. People keep asking us to make a chocolate with cheese. Actually, the make-up of blue cheese and chocolate is quite similar. I'm open to savoury flavours – like fresh thyme, Szechuan pepper and lime. That's because I worked in the main area in the kitchen as well as in pastry, where everything tends to be sweet.

The British have lost a taste for real flavours. We make a chocolate with fresh Moroccan mint, but because people are used to mint chocolates made with artificial mint flavourings, when they try our fresh mint chocolate, they don't recognise the flavour.

It's a very personal thing. The chocolates we create are the chocolates we like. I use the market to see if other people like them as well.

There's a place for McDonald's. And there's a place for a Michelin three-starred restaurant, too. In the middle, there's a whole grey area where restaurants and manufacturers make food really cheaply but they can get away with charging quite a high price.

People don't complain enough in this country. If they have a bad experience they'd rather keep quiet than do something about it. That approach is not going to get manufacturers to change their practices.

Shopping at the market is an education. This is where people learn about food – where it comes from and how it should really taste. It's a real challenge to change the way people think. But that's the joy of Borough Market – I think it's having an effect.

Chocolate Tart

Serves 10

The history of chocolate consumption is nearly as long as that of Borough Market itself. Savoured in Europe since the Spanish introduced it in the seventeenth century, the first 'chocolate house' opened in London in 1657, serving hot chocolate drinks – a precursor to the cafes of today. In 1847 sugar, cocoa powder and cocoa butter were combined to make solid chocolate. The rest, as they say, is history. This chocolate tart celebrates all that is best about good quality chocolate – it's adapted from a recipe by Sara-Jayne Stanes, author of *Chocolate: the Definitive Guide*, and is the ultimate treat.

PASTRY SHELL
85gm / 3oz plain flour and
45gm / 1oz cocoa powder,
sifted together
75gm / 3oz unsalted butter
30gm / 1oz ground almonds
55gm / 2oz caster sugar
1 large egg, lightly beaten

FILLING
225gm / 8oz bitter chocolate
55gm / 2oz unsalted butter
3 large eggs, separated
85gm / 3oz caster sugar
6 tblsp double cream
coffee

PASTRY SHELL

1 Butter and flour a 23cm x 2.5cm [9 inch x 1 inch] flan tin. Preheat oven to 200C / 400F gas 6.

2 To make the pastry, put all ingredients into a food processor and whizz for about 15 seconds – not more or it becomes greasy and will be tough. Make it into a ball with your hands. Cover and refrigerate for 30 minutes. Roll out thinly. Transfer to the tin and leave in the fridge for another 30 minutes. Line with foil and bake blind for 15 minutes. Remove from oven, take out the foil bake for 15 minutes.

FILLING

1 Melt chocolate and butter together. Cool slightly. Whisk the egg whites to soft peaks – don't over beat. Lightly whisk the egg yolks and sugar to a frothy stage. Stir in double cream and coffee. Add the chocolate and butte and stir gently. Fold in the beaten egg whites.

2 Tip the mixture into the tart case and spread with a spatula. Bake for 20–25 minutes. The tart should be very soft in the centre; it will firm up as it cools. Serve cold with a dollop of sour cream or ice cream.

tip Too many chocolate makers use cheap chocolate. I buy from the best chocolate suppliers in France: Valrhona or Chocolaterie de L'Opera. But it doesn't end there. I use cream from Normandy. If I'm making champagne truffles, I use real champagne, not marc de champagne. You can taste the **difference.** Gerard Coleman, L'Artisan du Chocolat

DRINK

The revival of small breweries across Britain is celebrated in the range of speciality beers on sale at the Borough Market. You will also find fine wines, vintage ports and other alcoholic specialities, as well as traditional ciders for drinking and cooking. The very best coffee, teas, fresh fruit juices and yogurt drinks complete the market's liquid lunch.

tip Real cider is great for use in cooking, it adds a fruity sharp flavour to sauces in place of white wine, deglazes the pan after browning meat and is perfect for making a gravy to go with roast pork dinners. You can also poach whole fish in cider. Barry Topp, New Forest Cider

tip We've got a wheat beer from Corsica called Pietra Colomba that's very unusual. It's flavoured with ginger, wild pine and an indigenous herb from Corsica. It gives you a dry flavour and is very good with Indian food. Richard Dinwoodie, Utobeer

Market thoughts

Carolyn Lucas
Local resident.

The market's transformed my life, it's a breath of fresh air. Borough was a dreadful place before, there was nowhere to shop and being in a wheelchair made life difficult.

I fell ill many years ago and have been in a wheelchair since then. It makes getting around a chore, and shopping a nightmare, but the relationships I have with the stallholders make buying food enjoyable.

I go every Saturday, it can be quite a long shopping expedition because I end up having chats with everybody. You certainly feel a sense of closeness and friendship with the various stallholders after a while.

Kevin Loe, from Turnips, and I do concerts together. If he starts singing at the market, I join in. We have a quartet called the Tabard Singers.

My husband, Tony, is the rector of St George the Martyr on Borough High Street. We moved to the area 13 years ago because of his work. Tony is retiring in 18 months, which means we'll have to move but I will come back to the market each week to do my shopping.

I don't like the idea of eating supermarket food. Shopping at the market means I know that the animals I eat had a happy life. The meat from Richard and Lizzy Vine at Wild Beef is so good that it requires little cooking.

It's unnatural to be a vegetarian. If you watch wildlife programs on television you can see that other animals kill each other for food in order to survive.

I'm very frugal. I come from a post-war generation, so I'm not used to eating luxury foods. You don't have to eat expensively to eat well. I can make a silverside of beef last for three meals.

My husband used to do all of the shopping, he went to Tesco in Surrey Quays. Now, I do it, it's entertaining. If I leave in a bad mood, I will come back happy.

I used to be in theatre. I was in *The Bill,* like everyone else. I worked at the Young Vic. But my health has not been so good so I no longer act, but I go to the theatre quite a lot.

I'm a jack of all trades and a master of none. I now work on the information desk at the Tate Modern, I also make jewellery – some of my pieces have been on display in Zandra Rhode's Fashion and Textile Museum and in the V&A.

My father couldn't believe it when I told him we were moving to Borough. He worked at Unilever for 35 years. To get to work each day he took a tram across Blackfriar's Bridge that had St George the Martyr on it.

My father was born on Jamaica Road, just off of Tooley Street. My maternal grandfather was a leatherworker in Bermondsey. My great granddad was a supervisor at Surrey Docks. So, if I have any roots, maybe they are here.

The bigger picture

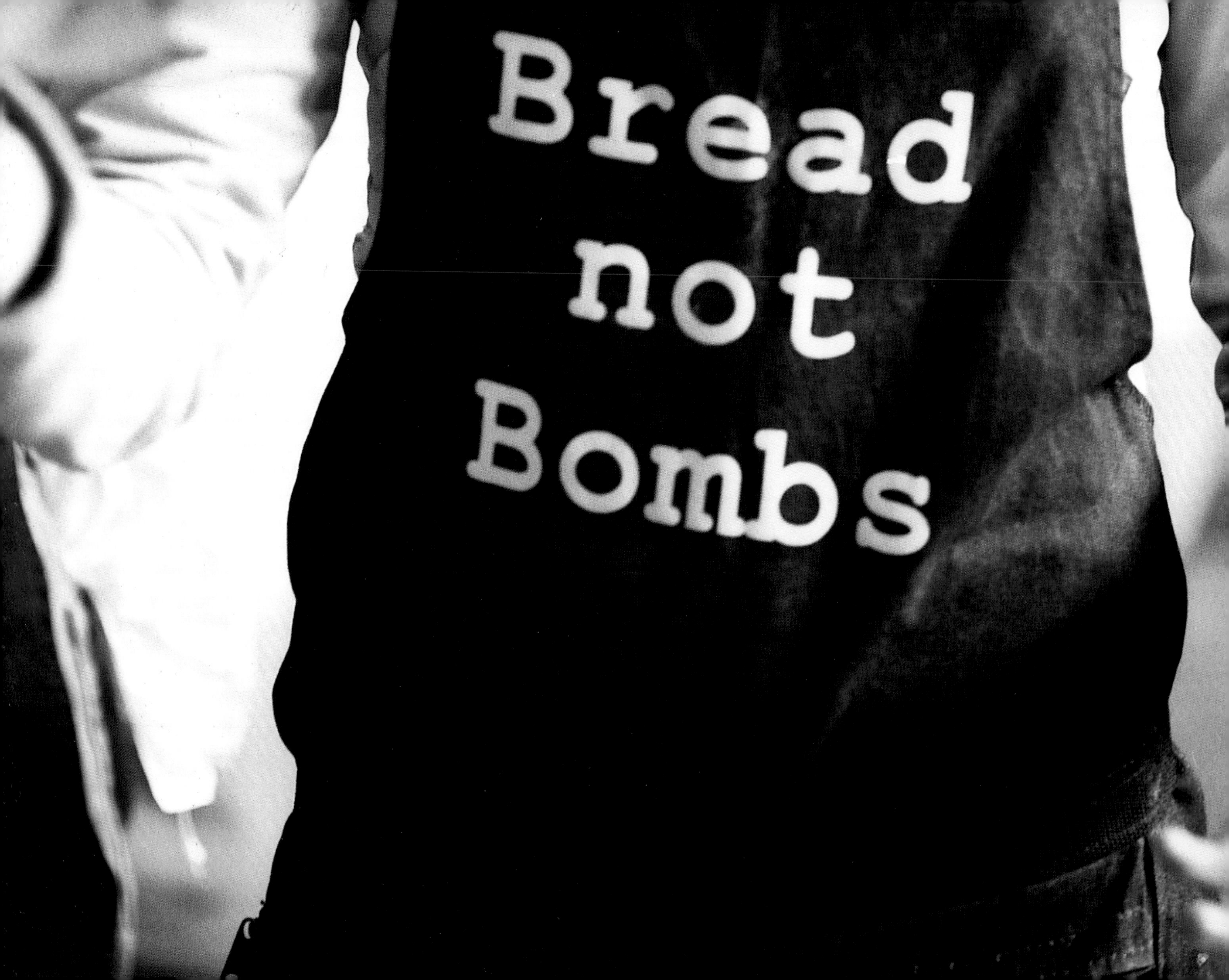
Bread
not
Bombs

THOUGHT FOR FOOD

BY SHEILA DILLON

In the mid '90s Britain received a rude awakening to the dangers of over-produced, low quality meat from the distressing images of cattle in the throes of Mad Cow Disease. In the intervening years a quiet revolution has become a battle cry: the health of the nation depends on the food we eat. But do Whitehall and Brussels really have our diet at heart?

You could say that Borough Market got its start in 1987 when the first glimmers appeared of the horror that was to be the BSE crisis. Up to that point campaigners for quality food, those concerned about the destruction of small food producers and the gradual takeover of the food trade by a small group of very large retailers, had been doing their worrying in front of a very small audience. If you were a small producer you knew which way the wind was blowing. But most of us, it seemed, had never had it so good: cheap food in profusion, in an ever increasing number of grand, one-stop stores – Aladdin's caves of bright choice, shopping made convenient beyond the dreams of our mothers or grandmothers. Even those with the lightest wallets could feel they were part of some marvellous, modern dream of plenty as they wandered the long wide aisles, considering the merits of vanilla cream ice lollies, yogurts with, without or semi-fatted in 18 flavours or fat-breasted chickens at 50p a 1lb. To question how such cheap plenty was possible seemed to most people to be just dog-in-the-manger-ish. Enjoy!

But then cows started to go mad on our television screens and it was a sickening sight. Though what was more sickening over the next ten years were the lies, obfuscations, spin and arrogance of the politicians in charge of our food supply, and of their foot soldiers: scientists, vets, doctors and civil servants. They vied with each other to reassure us that, as Dr Donald Acheson, the country's chief medical officer, said in 1990, there is "no risk associated with eating British beef." But, even while we were willing to give the boosters and spinners the benefit of the doubt, we could all see something that campaigners had been struggling to bring to the light for years – the lengths that agribusiness would go to increase their profit margins. We saw that these mad herbivores had been force-fed the dried and mashed up bodies of cows, sheep and chickens, along with chicken droppings and other dainties. Farmers didn't know what they were buying in their sacks of dried concentrates because the ministry of agriculture, fisheries and food had long ago given into the wishes of the feed industry and did not require the companies to list the feed ingredients on the bags. Sheep, chickens, cows or soya beans – it was all protein on the label. Even the most dedicated urbanite knew that this was not, as they said from Ullapool to Dover in a thousand radio and TV interviews, "natural". Numerous experts lectured us on the absurd naiveté of such a view, and millions of us ignored them. We'd seen what we'd seen and it was unnatural.

In May '95, 19 year-old Stephen Churchill died from the human variant of mad cow disease – and still the prime minister told us there was no evidence of a link between eating beef and getting variant CJD. But the tide was at the turn and the scientific experts and purveyors of economic efficiency could no longer count on mass unthinking acceptance of their point of view. 138 more deaths from vCJD concentrated the nation's mind. Cheapness was no longer, in itself, necessarily a good quality – the question now was, how did it get to be so cheap? It was a question the food industry didn't want asked, but there was nothing they could do to stop this new interest in the source of our food.

So suddenly, unexpectedly, out of the horror of BSE, came a strange good: a new space in Britain for the food worriers and campaigners and the real food nuts. The

WE ARE ONE OF
THE WORLD'S LEADERS IN
WHAT THE WORLD
HEALTH ORGANISATION CALLS
THE GLOBAL
"EPIDEMIC" OF OBESITY

media wanted to hear from them and increasing numbers of people wanted their advice on where to buy "safe" food. There were dozens who'd worked for years beneath the media radar: Tim Lang, founding director of the London Food Commission, was one. Now he had a platform for his analysis of the shoddiness, profiteering and corruption at work in our obscure and opaque food chain. Another was Randolph Hodgson. In 1979 he'd founded Neal's Yard Dairy in Covent Garden and shortly thereafter had set about his one-man campaign to save our traditional farmhouse cheeses and encourage new cheesemakers to set up – promising them a place in his shop if what they made was up to his high standards. The queues outside Neal's Yard grew longer and the Specialist Cheesemakers Association he'd helped found to head off MAFF's attempts to ban unpasteurised cheese, grew in numbers and influence.

And most crucially there was Henrietta Green. In the late '80s she'd compiled British Food Finds, the first ever list of our best foods, as a source for the food buying trade. But she then spent four fruitless years trying to persuade publishers that the general public was hungry for a similar book. In 1992, with the support of BBC Radio 4's *The Food Programme*, she found one, and in the following year her mass-market paperback *Food Lovers' Guide to Britain*, made available to everyone the riches of Britain's food culture. These were the producers who had survived the onslaught of the government's post-war cheap food policy, working mostly in isolation and against the grain of society, but now gathered together for all to see. We could buy, and they could exchange information, organise, lobby and begin to

take some public pride in what they were producing. Five years later, it was Henrietta with her second Food Lovers' Fair, bringing together the food producers in the guide, who gave the kick-start to Borough Market.

In the six years since that beginning at Borough there have been two parallel food narratives in Britain. The good tale has many strands: the growth of farmers' markets linking town and country to mutual benefit; the increasing influence of Borough Market as a model for city and town councils all over Britain, demonstrating that high quality food markets can help in regenerating run down urban centres. And that exciting people with tasty, real food can get them cooking again – and if you're cooking, you're eating better. Belfast, Leicester, Manchester and Bradford are just four cities that, as a result of contact with Borough, have turned around their markets.

All this has gone hand in hand with an increase in the number and quality of craft food producers. And the standards they've set have in turn put pressure on the big producers to raise their quality game. Marks & Spencer now not only sell just free-range eggs in their stores, they have a policy of only using free-range in their manufactured foods.... McDonald's sells organic milk in their children's meals .... Pret A Manger use only organic milk in all their hot drinks. Tesco and McDonalds are helping to finance some of Britain's most creative research into animal welfare at the Food Animal Initiative in Oxfordshire. It's a long list and it's not all driven by company public relations.

But the other tale of food in Britain is a darker one. The conditions in which small

EVERYTHING
ON THIS STALL
WAS HARVESTED
YESTERDAY
AND IS
ORGANIC

TOTAL ORGANICS
VEGETABLES THAT WONT BITE B

organic
herbs from heaven

ORGANIC
SPANISH OMELETTE
£2.50
PER SLICE

ORGANIC

BEEF
Native breeds
Naturally suckled
and grass rear
aste the diff

producers work continue to get more difficult. Regulations to control what they do – from Brussels and Whitehall – seem to be drawn up, introduced and implemented in a parallel universe to the one politicians inhabit when they're publicly lauding markets and exhorting farmers to diversify. Craft producers now work in a system of regulations almost totally unsuited to what they do and the foods they produce. It's a system set up to contain the risks inherent in a global system of food production and supply – one where there's a high turnover of labour, where piece workers know virtually nothing about the food they're handling and where they're paid no more than the minimum wage.

In countries with an old food culture, such as Italy, France and Spain, these rules are given a common-sense slant by vets and hygiene officials who know that if they wish to keep eating well they must work with small producers, not against them. Reporting for *The Food Programme* in the Paris region, I saw this in action when Simon Parkes and I visited a man much honoured as the producer of France's best andouillette (tripe sausages). We went with the region's chief vet, the equivalent of any British metropolitan council's chief environmental health officer. We saw, in the small, processing plant behind the master's shop in the Paris suburbs, how EU hygiene rules had been put in place without altering any of the traditional methods that made his sausages so sought after. And without involving him in crippling expense, either.

In May this year I travelled, again for *The Food Programme*, with Borough stallholders Peter Gott, Andrew Sharp and Richard Lancaster an official from Cumbria's Rural Regeneration office, to the French Pyrenees. The visit provided an even more graphic contrast between the way EU legislation is enforced in France and in the UK. A group of Pyreneean shepherds has recently been granted an 'appellation d'origine controlee' for their lamb and mutton. To get the appellation, which now gives them 1 euro per kilo more for their meat, they had to get an abattoir built in the mountains where they farm – and they'd succeeded. This was something that had eluded the Cumbrians, in spite of years of lobbying and desperate need. The Cumbrians were initially sceptical that their French counterparts could have achieved their goals honestly under EU rules, but three days of meetings with farmers, two mayors and several civil servants, all willing to open their books to us, convinced us all that that there'd been no underhand dealings in getting the new abattoir built. They'd achieved honestly what here is proving almost impossible.

The difference lay in the role of local councils, and in attitudes. Councils in rural France have real power and significant budgets and they use both in defence of local interests. In the Pyrenees, as in other parts of the country, local officials believe that local food is important both socially and economically. It keeps rural areas in good heart, providing jobs on farms and in secondary level businesses in butchers, epiceries, traiteurs and markets, and it's a big attraction for tourists, which again supports more jobs. So the communities in the region decided that they would guarantee the low-interest bank loan necessary to make up the 60 per cent of the abattoir cost not covered by the standard 40 per cent EU grant. As I sat in the

IN THE PYRENEES, AS IN OTHER PARTS OF FRANCE, LOCAL OFFICIALS BELIEVE THAT LOCAL FOOD IS IMPORTANT BOTH SOCIALLY AND ECONOMICALLY.

spring sunshine on the mountainside, with officials and farmers and my Cumbrian fellow travellers, eating lamb that had lived in the fields around us, along with the special white beans of the region, followed by local cheeses and tarts filled with blueberries – also grown on the mountainside – I saw another reason why the abattoir got built. Everyone there knows what good food is and they want to ensure that they, their children and their grandchildren will go on eating it. That's what we don't have in Britain and what Borough Market is helping to build again – a base of knowledgeable consumers. Food policy in this country is still for the most part created by men – and a few women – who eat badly and neither know nor care that that is what they're doing.

But policy makers have to care about the nation's health and that is getting dramatically worse. I won't rehearse the statistics here, but we are one of the world's leaders in what the World Health Organisation calls the global "epidemic" of obesity. We're also helping set the pace in numbers of people developing Type 2 diabetes (until recently called Adult-Onset diabetes, until our children started to develop it) and our cancer rates continue to rise. What people eat is key to solving all three health problems. For most of the past 15 years government departments and official quangos have tended to take a technical position on these problems: the solution will come by persuading people to eat food that has been manipulated to have less of the baddies: salt, sugar, fat. So we are encouraged to eat low-fat cheese, fatless yogurt, fibre enriched processed cereals, artificially sweetened drinks – in short the American diet. And until recently it seemed few of these policy makers had noticed that the fatless, sugarless, saltless American diet is a total disaster. In June 2004 *The Wall Street Journal* reported on an American Diabetic Association study of high school students in Texas, California and North Carolina which showed that by the age of 14, some 40 per cent were already showing signs of Type 2 diabetes which meant they either had high blood pressure, high cholesterol or blood-glucose abnormalities. At the same time the federal Centres for Disease Control said that of the 18.2 million Americans who have full-blown diabetes, 17 million have Type 2. As the Harvard economists David Cutler, Jesse Shapiro and Edward Glaeser had noted in their 2003 paper, "Why have Americans become more obese?", obesity is correlated with a level of regulation – the more protected local producers are, the harder it is for fast food merchants to get a hold in society, the thinner people are. Food quality, as the government is slowly and reluctantly beginning to recognise, is the issue.

So while we wait for policy makers to catch up with elementary good sense what can we do? It's very simple – buy local and ask what meat, milk and eggs are produced in free-range systems. And if you can afford it, buy organic. As journalist and food lover Dominic Prince recently proved in rural Dorset and central London, if you're buying real food – ingredients for cooking rather than processed, packaged food – it's cheaper to buy your food from local shops and markets than from the big retailers. In Dorset the identical shopping list cost him 43 per cent more at a well-known supermarket than it did when he bought his food locally, and buying locally took less time. So be good to yourself, shop well, eat well and get rich.

EVERYONE THERE
KNOWS WHAT GOOD FOOD IS
AND THEY WANT TO ENSURE THAT THEY,
THEIR CHILDREN AND THEIR
GRANDCHILDREN
WILL GO ON EATING IT.

Market thoughts

Mike Challenger
Local resident and artist and a dedicated fan of Borough Market.

I moved to Borough in 1976. I was looking for an artist's studio to rent because I'm a painter.

Space was cheap then. The area was certainly not the place people would want to come to. It had 'had its day' if you know what I mean. But it was thriving in terms of the market, which was wholesale then.

Change was utterly necessary. The market started to go downhill. Then along came Henrietta Green and her Food Lovers' Fair in November 1998, which ran for three days. More than 30,000 people came to Borough in just one weekend.

It's an amazing renaissance. Before, the market slept when everyone else was awake and was alive when they were asleep. Now they're very much up and thriving at the same time.

In the past 20 years over 150 feature films have been made in Borough. They use Park Street, where I live, a lot. My house was used in *Lock, Stock and Two Smoking Barrels*. The house where the gun-toting gangsters would meet: that's my house.

I couldn't figure out why they came here. I asked the film producers and they said it was because 'all the other streets in London are being mucked about with'. On Park Street all the windowpanes are original. The house frontages haven't been changed.

I'm a funny guy. I like the filming that goes on there. I'm a sucker for the creative process. My studio is not open now. I suffer from the rise in commercial leases, which is ironic because I was drawn to Borough because it was cheap.

The last show I did was in the mid-'90s. I did a lot of shows then. I exhibited alongside John Lennon in Germany – that was in my arrogant youth. I'd describe my art as geometric. I have some work in Tate Britain, but you have to ask to see it.

I was invited to Saudi Arabia just before the first Gulf War, to record the old city of Jeddah. When there was the threat of Railtrack wiping out half of the market I thought 'someone should record this area before it changes, too'. Then I thought, 'I could do that'. I've since created a number of paintings of the area.

Helena Bonham Carter stood behind me when I protested Railtrack's plans to railroad the area. *Howard's End* was filmed here. The London Film Commission actively backed our concerns. They were going to build a viaduct through the market. A lot of people would have lost their homes.

In Borough you have a stable, indigenous local environment of people who've lived here for ages. We all know each other. You can't even post a letter without having to say 'hello' to a dozen people. I love it.

SOUTHWARK SURROUNDS

BY JO FRENCH

The relationship between Southwark and the City of London is a historic tale of two contrasting cities living on opposite sides of the great River Thames. Feeding off one another for business and pleasure, this mutually dependent, yet essentially uneasy partnership, has been as long, complex and colourful as the tides of time.

Southwark is often described as London's first suburb, but it was surely on the south bank that weary and muddy-sandalled Romans of the mid-first century AD camped on the marshy islands and considered how and where to cross the river to the higher, drier, north side. Their choice ensured the future of both the South-work and Londinium and at the same time established a symbiotic, but sometimes uneasy, relationship between the two.

By 1206, the site the Romans had chosen formed the foundation of a new stone bridge. Travellers and goods from all over the south and east of England were funnelled up Long Southwark to this single crossing point. Narrow and uncomfortable as it was, traffic was often held up, and crossing by foot, though quicker, had its own hazards. In October 1664, Pepys was caught up in a coach jam on the bridge approach and retreated to an inn, the Beare at Bridge Foot. Unfortunately for him, when the jam cleared the coach was forced to go on without him... "So I fain to go through the dark and dirt over the bridge, and my leg fell in a deep hole broke on the bridge; but the constable standing there to keep people from it, I was ketched up, otherwise I had broke my leg...". The old bridge was not rebuilt until 1831, and soon after in 1836, London Bridge Station, the first railway terminus in London, brought more bridge traffic in the form of a black tide of city commuters, which streamed across the river twice a day.

Southwark grew fat on all this traffic jostling along the broad High Street to and from the bridge. Generations of travellers mustered here before journeying together down one of the roads that diverged near St George's Church, either south down Stane Street (Newington Street) or East along Watling Street to Kent, Canterbury and the channel ports (the Old Kent Road). The inns of Southwark did a roaring trade ministering to their needs with various standards of sleeping accommodation, food, drink and stabling. The inns were joined by taverns, such as the anonymous one where Pepys enjoyed a 'great dinner' in 1663, and drinking houses satisfying the leisure interests of the city and of Southwark. A written agreement dated 1319, concerns a tavern at Bridge Foot, leased to James Beauflur who agreed to buy his wines from the freeholder, ironically named Thomas Drinkwater. This was quite possibly the Beare.

From the Beare, numerous hostelries crowded the High Street, and the bustle and

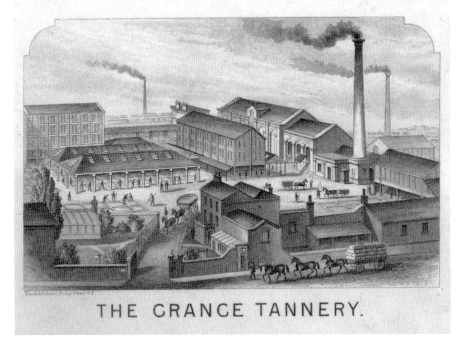

THE GRANGE TANNERY.

Far left: St Mary's Overie Dock, by Henry Dixon, 1881.
Left: The Grange Tannery, a typical example of industry in 19th century Southwark.
Right: Fire in Southwark, 1861.

THE GREAT FIRE IN SOUTHWARK: SCENE AT COTTON'S WHARF ON SUNDAY MORNING AT TWO O'CLOCK.

noise of travel, restless horses and grinding wheels filled the yards of renowned inns such as the King's Head, White Hart, George, Tabard, Queen's Head, Bull, Christopher, and Spurre. The Tabard or Talbot (rebuilt several times and demolished in 1875) was where Chaucer's assorted characters gathered before their long journey to Canterbury. Later, in the days of the turnpikes, gentlemen would head for these inns to catch long distance coaches, and the humbler members of society could seek out the carriers' carts. As Dickens wrote in *Pickwick Papers* in 1836: 'Great, rambling, queer old places they are, with galleries, and passages, and staircases, wide enough and antiquated enough to furnish materials for a hundred ghost stories….' As the railways stole the life blood of these great old inns, they turned to ghosts themselves, lurking in spirit behind the yard names of Borough High Street and rattling their notoriety in history and literature. Predictably, the drinking houses live on.

Although the travellers passing through Borough contributed to its fortunes, the transport of goods was an important element too. On the river, the 'legal' wharves of the north shore were reserved for high value goods, so cheap bulk goods and foodstuffs bound for the city headed for the south shore. Goods were unloaded and stored, before being moved by road on to the bridge approach to the city. It was also to Southwark that fruit, vegetables and hops came up from Kent and Sussex, and to Southwark that cattle and sheep and other animals made their way on the hoof along the drove roads from the east and south. All these goods, animals and people had always come to the same pinch point on the bridge approach, making it a natural site for a market. Around it grew associated trades such as shambles, butchers and wholesalers, many in fixed shops. This was the traditional and enduring strength of Borough Market – a food supply centre, located first on the bridge approach, then in Borough High Street, and from 1756 in the shadow of St Saviour's Church. With the Bridge House at one stage serving as a grain store for the 'City and Nation', especially in times of dearth, Borough practically controlled the food supply to London from the south and east.

Southwark was not only London's Larder. While the City developed as the strictly controlled and thriving commercial heart of the realm, its complex system of freedoms, privileges and livery companies never took hold south of the river. This

Opposite far left: A typical back street in 19th century Borough.
Opposite left: Borough High Street food shops.
This page right: Wilmott's Buildings, c.1900.
This page far right: A cheap lodging house in Tabard Street, behind St George's Church.

Left: The oldest operating theatre in Britain, in the roof space of the English Baroque Church, opposite St Thomas's Hospital.

was useful for London, as certain essential trades, undesirable in the city itself, could flourish nearby but out of nose and noise range. Southwark became London's workshop, servants' hall and backyard: a role that remained pretty constant for more than a thousand years. In 1598, the city tailor, John Stow, wrote a history and description of London including Southwark as Bridge Ward Without. He described Southwark's Bridge House as the store for the stone and timber for repairing the bridge, it also had 10 bread ovens and '...a fair brewhouse new built, for service of the city with beer'. These represented the bulky and offensive trades, relegated to Southwark from the earliest days. Other obvious ones were slaughtering, dyeing, and tanning. Richard Horwood's map of 1799 shows several timber yards, a sawyer's yard, rope walks (especially in Bermondsey), an iron foundry, turpentine factory, vinegar manufactory, skin yards and tanneries as well as numerous breweries on Bankside. It must have smelt delightful. Brewing brought with it the Kent hop trade, so Borough was home to the Hop Exchange (the building is still there) and various hop factors including W.H. LeMay at 67 Borough High Street. Timber merchants and coal merchants flourished in Southwark until well into the twentieth

century, as did the Victorian Phoenix Gas Works, itself succeeded by Sir Giles Gilbert Scott's Bankside Power Station of 1960 (now the impressive Tate Modern). The city, being on a constant alert of fire, also preferred trades such as glassblowing to be out of harm's way – south of the river was ideal. In consequence, over the centuries Southwark suffered more than its fair share of fires.

By 1598, developed Southwark extended half a mile to the west of the bridge, and half a mile to the east. The buildings also stretched for one mile south of London Bridge along Long Southwark as far as New Town (Newington). The Borough was wealthy, described as yielding '...more than any one City in England payeth, except the City of London'. There were several great houses in Borough especially for churchmen of Kent and Sussex, including the palaces of the bishops of Rochester and of Winchester (a fragment of which can still be seen on Clink Street). On the High Street itself, buildings grew tall, impressive and well appointed for the wealthier residents, but the back streets were poor, cramped and populous and remained so for hundreds of years. The majority of poor were no doubt honest workers in one of Southwark's industries, but it must have been temptingly easy for

criminal elements, characterised in the likes of Bill Sykes, to lose themselves in Southwark's misty alleys and rookeries. Comeuppance was to be expected, hence the cliché of a villain's demise in a muddy Thames creek which lasted well into twentieth century film and television.

It was an affront that the one 'privilege' extended to Southwark was for the Bankside stews or brothels. These were strictly controlled by a twelfth century statute (detailed by Stow at great length) until Henry VIII withdrew it. Needless to say, the trade endured. In 1720 the Reverend John Strype, updating Stow's survey, remained reticent on the subject, but in 1746, John Rocque the surveyor, marked an alley behind Stoney Street as 'The Whores' Nest.

With so many inns, brothels and entertainments on the south bank it is hardly surprising that Southwark gained a rather lawless reputation, but this did not totally explain the number of prisons. The Clink on Clink Street was a gaol for those who broke the peace on Bankside, and the Compter, in what had once been St Margaret's Church, was also for local felons convicted in its own court. The other prisons were foisted on Southwark, away from the city. The White Lion near St George's Church was administered and peopled by the courts of the county of Surrey. The King's Bench, small, airless and filled to overcrowded by Queen Elizabeth 1st, was notorious for the number of deaths from 'The Sickness of the House'. A new King's Bench was later built in Newington, and Horsemonger Lane

gaol was added to Southwark's collection in the 1790s. The Marshalsea, of which one massive wall remains, was also a royal prison, unpopular with the locals, as were the '...un-neighbourly and disdainful...' Marshal's men. At 12, Dickens had to visit his family at the Marshalsea where his father had been imprisoned for debt. The impression sank deep, and coloured his later writings with characters, atmosphere and tragedies.

As today, entertainments of sorts other than brothels and taverns were plentiful on the south bank. In the sixteenth century there was a Globe Theatre, now rebuilt on a nearby site on Bankside, the Rose Theatre, and the Swan. In addition '...there be two bear gardens, the old and new places, wherein be kept bears, bulls and other

beasts to be baited; as also mastiffs in several kennels, nourished to bait them.' By 1720 the site had been redeveloped, with smart houses as Bear Garden Square. Pepys often came over to Southwark to go walking across the fields to and from Lambeth, and in 1720 there was a recognised Thames walk along Bankside. It was not until 1750 that the building of Westminster Bridge drew developments, industries and smells further west to cover the fields, releasing Southwark forever from its London Bridge focus of development.

These days Southwark stretches from Blackfriars to Rotherhithe, and down to Dulwich, as just part of the great conurbation. The twentieth century had brought change, decline and decay, as the traffic in people, animals and goods drifted from

Borough High Street to main roads, tubes, railways and airports across the whole region. The noisy, bulky and smelly trades industrialised elsewhere, and power supply went underground. The small ships were replaced by containers unloading further east and boatmen were replaced by the bridges and the clippers. It is once again a pleasant walk along Bankside and on to Waterloo Bridge, but the river wharves have now gone in all but name. Only the tiny replica Golden Hinde at St Mary Overie's Dock remains to symbolise the flourishing river trade of the past.

So what is left in Southwark these days? Surprisingly, one could say more of the same, as if decline and change had been a short hiccup. Most is tidier, cleaner, safer and less smelly, with many old warehouses put to new uses such as antique stores supporting Bermondsey antique market, or smart homes and offices. Yet St. Saviour's, now Southwark's own cathedral, can still be glimpsed through the buildings of Borough Market, and its bells heard from afar. Calvert's Buildings on the High Street, Guy's Hospital, one wing of The George, The Anchor, Cardinal's Cap Alley, Hopton Street Almshouses, St Thomas's Church with its old operating theatre, the Hop Exchange and Borough Market, are all still there. Galleries, theatres and museums are probably more numerous than ever. Shakespeare's Globe, National Theatre, OXO Tower gallery & restaurant, HMS Belfast, Cuming Museum, Clink Museum, Rose Theatre, the Design Museum, Fashion & Textile Museum, Imperial War Museum, not to mention Tower Bridge with its walkways and engine rooms.

On the High Street many plots are tall and slim and shouldered together as they always were, despite rebuilding. But this is just fabric. Beneath, the bones of Southwark are the same. It is fighting unemployment and poverty in the same way as ever – as a leisure area and food supply centre for London. Although inns and taverns are fewer today, Pepys would still be able to enjoy a 'great dinner' in one of Southwark's restaurants, or take an ale or coffee in one of the numerous pubs, bars or cafés. And at the heart is still the Borough Market, drawing towards it not just produce from Kent and Sussex, but from all over the country and the world. Supermarket distribution systems undermined it, but there it is as large as life, newly refurbished and burgeoning once again. With numerous small shops consolidating the food specialism, the area as it is today is the epitome of what Borough has always done best for London.

MARKET TRADERS' DIRECTORY

Applebee's Fish
Graham Applebee
✉ Stoney Street, London SE1 9AA
☎ 07990 578883
✳ Fresh fish and shellfish.

Apulia Blend
Danilo Manco
✉ Unit PO3, Acton Business Centre,
School Road, London NW10 6TD
☎ 020 8961 8885
@ apuliablend@yahoo.co.uk
🖥 www.apuliablend.com
✳ Italian olive oils and balsamic vinegars.

Arabica
Jad Alunis
✉ 5 Selsdon Road, London SE27 0PQ
☎ 07974 937931
✳ Middle Eastern foodstuffs, take-away
falafel kebabs.

Artisan Foods
Klaus Kuhnke
✉ Arch 105, Cable Street, London E1 2LY
☎ 020 7702 3939
@ klaus@artisanfoods.co.uk
🖥 www.artisanfoods.co.uk
✳ Cakes, savoury and sweet pastries, take-
away hot sandwiches and soups.

Aunt Alice Puddings
Nancy Mahon
✉ Trading at Borough Market, London SE1
☎ 020 7798 8756
🖥 www.auntalice.com
✳ Hand made steamed dessert puddings.

Banana Store
✉ 1 Cathedral Street, London SE1 9DE
☎ 020 7357 9735
✳ Bar, diner and gallery.

Baxters Fruiterers
Leonard Baxter
✉ Stoney Street, London SE1 9AH
☎ 020 7403 0311
✳ Take-away barbecued steak sandwiches,
chips, crepes, ice cream, teas and coffees.

Bedales Gallery
✉ 4 Bedale Street, London SE1 9AL
☎ 020 7357 0665
✳ Art gallery.

Bedales Ltd
Erin Costello and Arnaud Compas
✉ 5 Bedale Street, Borough Market,
London SE1 9AL
☎ 020 7403 8853
@ arnaud@bedalestreet.com
🖥 www.BedaleStreet.com
✳ Fine wines and food.

Booth's Flowers
✉ 15 - 16 Stoney St, London SE1 9AD
☎ 020 7378 8666
@ lboothltd@aol.com
✳ Flowers.

L. Booth Ltd
Anthony Booth
✉ 15 - 16 Stoney St, London SE1 9AD
☎ 020 7378 8666
@ lboothltd@aol.com
✳ Wild mushrooms and seasonal fruits and
vegetables.

Borough Cheese Company
Dominic Coyte
✉ Trading at Borough Market, London SE1
☎ 07903 820605
✳ Specialising in Comté cheese, a hard
cow's milk cheese made in the Franche-
Comté region. Style similar to Gruyère.

Borough Wines Ltd
Muriel Chatel
✉ Unit 3k, Oslo House West,
67 Felstead Street, London E9 5LG
☎ 0870 2418890
@ info@boroughwines.co.uk
🖥 www.boroughwines.co.uk
✳ Wines from the family vineyard and
around the world.

A. & W. Bourne
Martin Bourne
✉ Borough Market, London SE1
☎ 020 7407 1909
✳ Vegetable wholesaler and retail trader.

H.S. Bourne
John Bourne
✉ The Bank, Malpas, Cheshire SY14 7AL
☎ 01948 770214
@ contact@hsbourne.co.uk
🖥 www.hsbourne.co.uk
✳ Choice traditional Cheshire cheese and
soft cheeses.

The Richard Bramble Collection
Richard Bramble
✉ 56b Vauxhall Grove, London SW8 1TB
☎ 020 7587 1471
@ info@richardbramble.com
🖥 www.richardbramble.com
✳ Hand made ingredient prints, Limoges
porcelain ceramics, tablemats, glass
boards, coasters, aprons and prints of the
market all by artist Richard Bramble.

Brindisa Spanish Foods
Monika Linton
✉ 32 Borough Market, London SE1 9AH
☎ 020 7407 1036
@ retail@brindisa.com
🖥 www.brindisa.com
✳ High quality Spanish foods and artisan
products sourced from all over Spain.

Brown & Forrest
Michael Brown
✉ Bowdens Farm, Hambridge,
Somerset TA10 0BP
☎ 01458 250875
@ brownforrest@btinternet.com
🖥 www.smokedeel.co.uk
✳ Smoked meat, game, fish and cheese.

Burnt Sugar
Justine Cather and Colin Cather
- ✉ 16 Manor Road, Beverley HU17 7BY
- ☎ 01482 863887
- @ info@burntsugar.co.uk
- 🖥 www.burntsugar.co.uk
- ✳ Toffee, fudge, ice cream, sugar confectionary, candy and lollipops.

C & C Fruits
Peter Fowler
- ✉ Borough Market, London SE1
- ☎ 020 7403 4416
- ✳ Vegetable wholesaler.

Cartwright Bros
David & Martin Cartwright
- ✉ 5 Bedale Street, Borough Market, London SE1 9AL
- ☎ 020 7403 8853
- @ mail@bedalestreet.com
- 🖥 www.BedaleStreet.com
- ✳ Fine wines, champagnes, ports and sherries.

Chegworth Valley Apple Juice
David Deme
- ✉ Water Lane Farm, Chegworth, Harrietsham, Maidstone, Kent ME17 1DE
- ☎ 01622 859272
- @ info@chegworthvalley.com
- 🖥 www.chegworthvalley.com
- ✳ Orchard fruits, fruit pies, juices, take-away juice in cups and during the summer: soft fruits, berries, etc.

& Clarke's
Paul Headford
- ✉ 122 & 124 Kensington Church Street, London W8 4BH
- ☎ 020 7229 2190
- @ shop@sallyclarke.com
- ✳ Home made breads, savoury tarts, jams, chutney, relishes, chocolate truffles and more.

Clean Bean
Neil McLennan
- ✉ 170 Brick Lane, London E1 6RU
- @ cleanbean@ssba.info
- ✳ Soya based products, primarily fresh and marinaded tofu (smokey, sesame & ginger, and 5-spice).

Cool Chile Co
Simon Kiddell
- ✉ Unit 7, Buspace Studio, Conlan Street, London W10 5AP
- ☎ 0870 9021145
- @ simon@coolchile.co.uk
- 🖥 www.coolchile.co.uk
- ✳ Fresh and dried chillies, salsas, sauces, take-away Mexican dishes.

Court Lodge Organics
Marian and David Harding
- ✉ Court Lodge Farm, Watting, Nr Hailsham, East Sussex BN27 1RY
- ☎ 01323 832150
- @ info@courtlodgeorganics.co.uk
- 🖥 www.courtlodgeorganics.co.uk
- ✳ Yogurt based smoothies and pouring yogurts, made with organic milk from own pedigree herd and other dairy products.

Dark Sugars
Fatou Mendy
- ✉ 224 Grove Green Road, Leytonstone, London E9 7HD
- ☎ 020 8257 3657
- 🖥 www.darksugars.co.uk
- ✳ Home made chocolates, cakes, tarts and truffles.

De Gustibus
Paul O'Brien
- ✉ 6 Southwark Street, London SE1 1TQ
- ☎ 020 7407 3625
- 🖥 www.degustibus.co.uk
- ✳ Breads, pastries, take-away sandwiches.

Denhay Farms
Amanda Streatfeild
- ✉ Broadoak, Bridport, Dorset DT6 5NP
- ☎ 01308 458963
- @ sales@denhay.co.uk
- 🖥 www.denhay.co.uk
- ✳ Air-dried ham, bacon, sausage, gammon and cheese. (Attends market every third Saturday of month.)

Dingle Peninsula Cheese
Maja Binder & Olivier Beaujouan
- ✉ Kilcummin Beg, Castlegregory, Co Kerry
- 🖥 www.corleggy.com
- ✳ Irish cheeses and seaweed products.

The Dorset Blueberry Company
David Trehane
- ✉ 352 Hampreston, Wimborne, Dorset BH21 7LX
- ☎ 01202 579342
- @ info@dorset-blueberry.co.uk
- 🖥 www.dorset-blueberry.co.uk
- ✳ Dorset blueberries and blueberry products, hand made jams, chutneys, mustards and sauces.

Dupond's Bakery Ltd
Paul Rhodes
- ✉ Cannon Wharf Business Centre, 35 Evelyn Street, London SE8 5RT
- ☎ 020 7237 5577
- @ post@dupondsbakery.com
- ✳ Traditionally and hand crafted French breads and pastries.

East Teas
Alex Fraser & Tim d'Offray
- ✉ 7 Aylwin Estate, Grange Walk, London SE1 3DU
- ☎ 020 7394 0226
- @ alex@eastteas.com
- 🖥 www.eastteas.com
- ✳ Traditional East Asian teas and tea utensils.

Elsey & Bent
Peter Fowler
- ✉ Units 4-11, Stoney Street, London SE1
- ☎ 020 7407 1166
- ✳ Fruit, vegetables and salad.

England Preserves
Sky Cracknell and Kai Knutsen
✉ Unit 4, Marlowe Business Centre, Batavia Road, London SE14 6BQ
☎ 020 8692 0806
@ sky@englandpreserves.demon.co.uk
✳ Various preserves and specialising in quince cheese.

FarmerSharp.Co.UK
Andrew Sharp
✉ Diamond Buildings, Pennington Lane, Lindal in Furness, Cumbria LA12 0LA
☎ 01229 588299
@ farmersharp@yahoo.co.uk
💻 www.farmersharp.co.uk
✳ Herdwick lamb and mutton, Galloway beef, Pink veal and air-dried mutton and mutton salamis.

Farmhouse Direct
David Kitson
✉ Long Ghyll Farms, Brock Close, Bleasdale, Preston PR3 1UZ
☎ 01995 61799
@ info@farmhousedirect.com
💻 www.farmhousedirect.com
✳ Highland beef, Blackface lamb and associated products.

Feng Sushi
✉ 13 Stoney Street, London SE1 9AD
☎ 020 7407 8744
💻 www.fengsushi.co.uk
✳ Japanese foods, eat in or take-away.

Fern Verrow Vegetables
Jane Scotter
✉ Fern Verrow Vegetables, St Margarets, Herefordshire HR2 0QF
☎ 01981 510288
@ fernverrow@btopenworld.com
✳ Bio-dynamic vegetables, and organic meats, eggs and honey (seasonal).

fish!
✉ Cathedral Street, Borough Market, London SE1 9AL
☎ 020 7836 3236
@ borough@fishdiner.co.uk
💻 www.fishdiner.co.uk
✳ Seafood restaurant.

Flour Power City
Matthew Jones
✉ Unit 5B, Juno Way, Elizabeth Industrial Estate, Surrey Quays, London SE14 5RW
☎ 020 8691 2288
@ info@flourpowercity.com
💻 www.flourpowercity.com
✳ Organic breads, croissants, chocolate brownies, cakes, muffins and savouries.

The Fresh Olive Co
Christabel and Camilla Clark
✉ Trading at Borough Market, London SE1
☎ 020 7370 7209
@ christabelclark@hotmail
💻 www.fresholive.co.uk
✳ Olives and olive oil, arborio rice, balsamic vinegar, garlic, pickles and semi-dried tomatoes, pesto sauce, harrissa, black tapenades and little olive trees.

Furness Fish and Poultry
Leslie Salisbury
✉ Stockbridge Lane off Daltongate, Ulverston, Cumbria LA12 7BG
☎ 020 7378 8899
@ furnessfish@yahoo.com
✳ Fish, shellfish, wild mussels, rod caught wild sea bass and home made potted shrimp. Award winning haggis and wild venison.

Fusebox
✉ 12 Stoney Street, London SE1 9AD
☎ 020 7407 9888
@ anyone@fuseboxfoods.com
💻 www.fuseboxfoods.com
✳ Pan-Asian lunch boxes and salads inspired by the East and Pacific Rim and oriental groceries.

Gamston Wood Ostriches
Susan & James Farr
✉ Gamston Wood Farm, Upton Retford, Nottinghamshire DN22 0RB
☎ 01777 838858
@ sales@gamstonwoodostriches.co.uk
💻 www.gamstonwoodostriches.co.uk
✳ Raw ostrich meat cut to order, hand made ostrich burgers, grills, meatballs and sausages made fresh on the farm weekly. Ostrich burgers and minute steaks cooked on the stall.

The Garlic Farm
Colin Boswell
✉ Mersley Farm, Mersley Lane, Newchurch, Sandown, Isle of Wight PO36 0NR
☎ 01983 865378
@ colin@thegarlicfarm.co.uk
💻 www.thegarlicfarm.co.uk
✳ Garlic and garlic products.

Gastronomica
Marco Vineis
✉ Unit 9, Parmiter Industrial Estate, Parmiter Street, London E2 9HZ
☎ 020 8980 5005
@ gastronomica2000@aol.com
✳ Italian cheeses and charcuterie.

German Wurst & Deli
Michael Ristau
✉ 127 Central Street, London EC1V 8AP
☎ 020 7250 1322
@ info@germandeli.co.uk
💻 www.germandeli.co.uk
✳ German sausages and groceries, take-away German sausages.

The Ginger Pig
Timothy Wilson
✉ Borough Market, Southwark Street, London SE1
☎ 020 7403 4721
✳ Fresh meat and poultry, sausages, bacon and seasonal game.

The Globe
✉ Bedale Street, London SE1
✳ Public House.

Gorwydd Farm Cheese
Martin Trethowan
✉ Gorwydd Farm, Llanddewi Brefi, Tregaron, Ceredigion SY25 6NY Wales
☎ 01570 493516
@ enquiries@trethowansdairy.co.uk
✳ Specialising in Caerphilly cheese. Trethowan's Gorwydd Caerphilly is a mature caerphilly made to a traditional recipe, using raw unpasteurised milk and GM-free vegetarian rennet.

The Greek Connection
Peter De Maar
✉ Trading at Borough Market, London SE1
☎ 020 8694 8067
@ petethegreek@operamail.com
✳ Greek foodstuffs, take-away kebabs.

Greenhouse Florists
Lila Bryan
✉ 1 Bedale Street, London SE1 9AL
☎ 020 7403 6304
✳ Flowers.

Richard Haward Oysters
Richard Haward
✉ The Company Shed, 129 Coast Road, West Mersea, Colchester CO5 8PA
☎ 01206 383284
@ richard@oysters.u-net.com
🖥 www.richardhawardoysters.co.uk
✳ Colchester Native and rock oysters.

Hobbs Barbershop
Mike Hobbs
✉ Borough Market, London SE1
✳ Barbers.

Hobbs Pie and Mash
Julie Hobbs
✉ 6 Bedale Street, London SE1
✳ Pie and mash, jellied eels, hot filled baguettes, sandwiches, teas and coffees.

Isle of Wight Tomatoes
Jeff MacDonald
✉ Main Road, Hale Common, Arreton, Isle of Wight PO30 3AR
☎ 01983 866907
@ isleofwhitetomatoes@btopenworld.com
✳ Tomatoes and tomato products from the Isle of Wight.

Jubilee Cafe
✉ Borough Market, London SE1
☎ 020 7407 0557
✳ English breakfasts, sandwiches, teas and coffees.

Konditor & Cook
✉ 10 Stoney Street, London SE1 9AD
☎ 020 7407 5100
@ stoneystreet@konditorandcook.com
🖥 www.konditorandcook.com
✳ Cakes, pastries, take-away meals, teas and coffees.

L'artisan du Chocolat
Gerard Coleman
✉ 89 Lower Sloane Street, London SW1W 8DA
☎ 020 7824 8365
@ order@artisanduchocolat.com
🖥 www.artisanduchocolat.com
✳ Hand made chocolates using only high quality natural ingredients and artisan rather than mass production techniques.

Le Marche du Quartier
Stephen Harrison
✉ 5 Bedale St, London SE1 9AL
@ stephen@lemarcheduquartier.com
🖥 www.lemarcheduquartier.com
✳ French food and wines.

Loco Pronto
✉ Cathedral Street, London SE1 9ED
☎ 020 7407 3801
✳ Take-away pizzas and Italian Breads.

London Honey Company
Steven Benbow & Jill Mead
✉ Trading at Borough Market, London SE1
☎ 020 7771 9152
@ info@beesplease.co.uk
🖥 www.beesplease.co.uk
✳ Honey from the rooftop gardens, gardens and parks of London's boroughs.

Long Crichel Bakery
Jamie Campbell
✉ Long Crichel, Wimborne, Dorset BH21 5JU
☎ 01258 830852
@ info@longcrichelbakery.co.uk
🖥 www.longcrichelbakery.co.uk
✳ Hand crafted organic breads and cakes baked in a woodfired oven.

Maison Bertaux
Michele Wade
✉ 28 Greek Street, Soho, London W1D 5DQ
☎ 020 7437 6007
✳ Cakes, croissants and pastries.

Maria's Market Cafe
Maria Moruzzi
✉ Stoney Street, London SE1
✳ English breakfasts, sandwiches, teas and coffees and Maria's famous bubble & squeak.

The Market Garden
Steve Lang
✉ 5 Stoney Street London SE1
☎ 07786 260536
✳ Pot plants and flowers.

Mid-Devon Fallow
Peter Kent
✉ Keyethern Farm, Hatherleigh, Okehampton, Devon EX20 3LG
☎ 01837 810028
@ mdf999@aol.com
✳ Fallow venison from the West Country.

Monmouth Coffee
Anita Le Roy
✉ 2 Park St, London SE1 9AB
☎ 020 7645 3560
@ beans@monmouthcoffee.co.uk
🖥 www.monmouthcoffee.co.uk
✳ Coffee beans, coffee and pastries.

Mrs Bassa's Indian Kitchen
M. Bassa
✉ Trident Business Centre, 89 Bickersteth Road, Tooting, London SW17 9SH
✳ Indian chutneys and sauces, take-away Indian snacks.

Mrs Kings Pork Pies
Ian Hartland
✉ Unit 30, High Hazles Road, Manvers Business Park, Cotgrave, Nottinghamshire NG12 3JW
☎ 0115 9894101
✳ Hand made Melton Mowbray pork pies.

The Natural Smoothie Co
Liz Mc Micken
✉ Violet Cottage, Laundry Road, Apethorpe, Northamptonshire PE8 5DQ
☎ 01780 470812
@ thenaturaljuice@hotmail.com
💻 www.thenaturalsmoothieco.com
✳ Take-away smoothies and juices and creator of social enterprise project to bring natural produce (frozen smoothies) into school childrens' diets for the price of a soft drink.

Neal's Yard Dairy
Randolph Hodgson
✉ 6 Park Street, London SE1 9AB
☎ 020 7645 3554
@ anne@nealsyarddairy.co.uk
💻 www.nealsyarddairy.co.uk
✳ Cheese and dairy products.

New Forest Cider
Barry Topp
✉ Littlemead, Pound Lane, Burley, Ringwood, Hampshire BH24 4ED
☎ 01425 403589
@ newforestcider@msn.com
💻 www.newforestcider.co.uk
✳ Cider, perry, apple juice, liqueurs, Somerset cider brandy and apple aperitif, take-away cider in glasses.

Northfield Farm Ltd
Rupert Titchmarsh
✉ Northfield Farm, Wissendine Lane, Cold Overton, Oakham, Rutland LE15 7QF
☎ 01664 474271
@ jan@northfieldfarm.com
💻 www.northfieldfarm.com
✳ Beef, pork and lamb. Traditional and rare breeds.

The Nut Man
Saied Saiedpour
✉ 6 Malvern Way, Ealing, London W13 8EB
☎ 020 8961 8686
@ info@nutman.co.uk
💻 www.cranberryuk.com
✳ A large variety of nuts, chocolates and dried fruit.

The Olive Garden
Vahid Moshtagh
✉ Trading at Borough Market, London SE1
✳ Olives, olive oil and soaps, Feta cheese, artichoke hearts, pesto sauce, tapenades, harrissa, sun-dried tomatoes.

Pays D'auge Fromages
Yann & Franck LeBlais
✉ 12 Clevedon Road, Twickenham, London TW1 2HU
☎ 020 8607 9762
✳ French cheeses.

Pots for Tots Ltd
Michael Corden
✉ Unit WHE 112, Wandsworth Business Village, 3-9 Broomhill Road, London SW18 4JQ
☎ 0845 4500875
@ info@potsfortots.co.uk
💻 www.potsfortots.co.uk
✳ Fresh organic toddler food.

Real France
Alex Cheesman
✉ 43 Borough Market, London SE1 9AH
☎ 020 7863 4410
✳ Echiré dairy products and specialist quality French foods.

Repro Image
Dave Mills
✉ 3 Bedale Street, London SE1 9AL
☎ 020 7403 0802
✳ Reprographic shop.

Roast
Iqbal Wahhab
✉ Floral Hall, Borough Market, London SE1
💻 www.roast-restaurant.com
✳ British cuisine.

G. Rowe Mushrooms
Geoff Rowe
✉ 64 Borough Market, London SE1 9AH
☎ 020 7407 9051
✳ Vegetable wholesaler.

Sardinia Organic
Enrico & Stefano Chessa
✉ Unit P03, Acton Business Centre, School Road, London NW10 6TD
☎ 020 8961 8885
@ info@sardiniaorganic.co.uk
💻 www.villanovafood.com
✳ Sardinian foodstuffs, Pecorino cheeses and Sardinian charcuterie.

Scandelicious
Anna Mosesson
✉ 4 Beaconsfield Rd, Aldeburgh, Suffolk IP15 5HF
☎ 01728 452880
@ anna@scandelicious.co.uk
💻 www.scandelicious.co.uk
✳ Scandinavian specialities.

Seldom Seen Farm
Robert Symington
✉ Seldom Seen Farm, Billesdon, Leicestershire LE7 9FA
☎ 0116 2596742
✳ At market seasonally. Late October for five weeks selling geese and three-bird roasts. In the spring for 12 weeks (February-April) selling boned and stuffed chicken and duck.

Shellseekers
Darren Brown
✉ Ten Acres, Conygar, Broadmayne, Dorset DT2 8LX
☎ 07074 104607
@ shellseekers@talk21.com
✳ Fresh fish, shellfish, take-away cooked seafood dishes.

Shipp and Sons
John Rich
✉ 4 Park Street, London SE1
☎ 020 7407 2692
✳ Electrical goods and contract electricians.

Silka Restaurant
✉ 6 - 8 Southwark Street, London SE1 1TL
☎ 020 7378 6161
@ hannan61@hotmail.com
🖥 www.silka.co.uk
✳ Indian restaurant.

Sillfield Farm
Peter Gott
✉ Sillfield Farm, Endmoor, Kendal, Cumbria LA8 0HZ
☎ 015395 67609
@ enquiries@sillfield.co.uk
🖥 www.sillfield.co.uk
✳ Wildboar, rare breed pork and bacon, unpasteurised cheese and hams.

A. Sugarman
Andrew Sugarman
✉ Stand 55, Borough Market, London SE1
@ alisonsugarman@aol.com
✳ Fruit and vegetable wholesaler and retail trader.

Sweet
Sebastian Wind
✉ Unit 4, 19-21 Payne Road Studios, London E3 2SP
☎ 020 7713 6777
@ info@sweetdesserts.co.uk
🖥 www.sweetdesserts.co.uk
✳ Cakes, pastries and savouries.

Tapas Brindisa
Monika Linton
✉ 18-20 Southwark Street, London SE1 1TJ
☎ 020 7357 8880
@ monikal@brindisa.com
✳ Spanish tapas bar. Lunch and dinner menus (open for breakfast on market trading days). Charcuterie and hand carved hams to take away from the restaurant's jamonería.

Ted's Veg (R.H. Dawson)
Ted Dawson
✉ West Virginia, West End, Benington, Boston, Lincolnshire PE22 0EJ
☎ 07931 765348
@ reevted@aol.com
✳ Specialise in seasonal globe artichokes and baby leaf salad, vegetables and some fruit.

Temptings
P. Sandhu
✉ 6 Uplands Ave, Hitchin, Hertfordshire SG4 9NH
☎ 01462 433600
✳ Specialise in pickles and chutney.

Jayne Thomas Farm Foods
Jayne Thomas
✉ Buttinghill, Hook Lane, West Hoathly, West Sussex RH19 4PT
☎ 01342 810125
@ jayne@duveen.co.uk
✳ Specialising in selling Daylesford organic Cheddar, traditionally made on the farm using unpasteurised milk and animal rennet.

Total Organics
Garry Greenland
✉ Stand 21-23 Borough Market, London SE1 9AH
☎ 020 7357 8537
✳ Organic vegetarian products, organic vegetables and juice bar.

Turnips
F & C Foster
✉ 43 Borough Market, London SE1 9AH
☎ 020 7357 8356
@ fred@turnipsdist.co.uk
✳ Fruit and vegetable wholesaler and retail trader.

Utobeer
Mike Hill & Richard Dinwoodie
✉ P.O Box 30053, London SE1 6XT
☎ 020 7394 8601
@ admin@utobeer.co.uk
🖥 www.utobeer.co.uk
✳ Large selection of beer and spirits (in bottles).

Wild Beef
Richard & Lizzie Vines
✉ Hillhead Farm, Chagford, Devon TQ13 8DY
☎ 01647 433433
✳ Beef, (native breeds - Welsh Blacks, North and South Devons), grass fed and four weeks hung. Devon cream, artisan mustard, relishes and honey.

Wild Wood Groves
Ruth Hajioff
✉ PO Box 33146 London NW3 7FS
☎ 020 8458 2738
@ ruth@wildwoodgroves.com
🖥 www.wildwoodgroves.com
✳ Argan cold-pressed virgin oil and a range of Argan skin care products. Saffron from the Atlas mountains and Moroccan spices.

Wyndham House Poultry
Lee Mullet
✉ 2-3 Stoney Street, London SE1 9AA
☎ 020 7403 4788
✳ Poultry and game.

Traders by category

Alcoholic Beverages
Bedales Ltd
Borough Wines
Cartwright Bros
Le Marche du Quartier
New Forest Cider
Utobeer

Artwork
The Richard Bramble Collection

Beverages, Juices & Soups
Court Lodge Organics
East Teas
Monmouth Coffee Company
The Natural Smoothie Co

Breads, Cakes & Pastries
Artisan Foods
& Clarke's
De Gustibus
Dupond's Bakery
Flour Power City
Konditor & Cook
Long Crichel Bakery
Maison Bertaux
Sweet

Cheeses
Borough Cheese Company
H.S. Bourne
Dingle Peninsula Cheese
Gorwydd Farm Cheese
Neal's Yard Dairy
Pays D'auge Fromages
Jayne Thomas Farm Foods

Children's Speciality Food
Pots for Tots Ltd

Confectionary
Burnt Sugar
Dark Sugars
L'artisan du Chocolat

Desserts & Puddings
Aunt Alice Puddings

Fish & Shellfish
Applebee's Fish
fish!
Furness Fish and Poultry
Richard Haward Oysters
Shellseekers

Flowers
Booth's Flowers
Greenhouse Florists
The Market Garden

Fruit & Vegetables
Chegworth Valley Apple Juice
Fern Verrow Vegetables
The Garlic Farm
Isle of Wight Tomatoes
Ted's Veg (R.H Dawson)
Total Organics
Turnips

Herbs & Spices
Cool Chile Co

International Foods
Apulia Blend
Arabica
Brindisa Spanish Foods
Clean Bean
Feng Sushi
The Fresh Olive Co
Fusebox
Gastronomica
German Wurst & Deli
The Greek Connection
Mrs Bassa's Indian Kitchen
The Olive Garden
Real France
Sardinia Organic
Scandelicious
Wild Wood Groves

Meat, Game & Poultry
Brown & Forrest
Denhay Farms
FarmerSharp.Co.UK
Farmhouse Direct
Gamston Wood Ostriches
The Ginger Pig
Mid-Devon Fallow
Northfield Farm Ltd
Seldom Seen Farm
Sillfield Farm
Wild Beef
Wyndham House Poultry

Nuts, Dried Fruits & Cereals
The Nut Man

Pies, Pastries & Rolls
Hobbs Pie and Mash
Mrs Kings Pork Pies

Preserves & Chutney
The Dorset Blueberry Company
England Preserves
London Honey Company
Temptings

Fruit & Vegetable Wholesalers
L. Booth Ltd
A. & W. Bourne
Baxters Fruiterers
C & C Fruits
Elsey & Bent
G. Rowe Mushrooms
A. Sugarman

Shops, Cafés, Pubs & Restaurants
Applebee Fish
Banana Store
Bedales
Bedales Gallery
De Gustibus
Feng Sushi
fish!
Fusebox
The Globe
Greenhouse Florists
Hobbs Barbershop
Jubilee Cafe
Konditor & Cook
Loco Pronto
Maria's Market Cafe
Monmouth Coffee Company
Neal's Yard Dairy
Repro Image
Roast
Shipp and Sons
Silka Restaurant
Tapas Brindisa
Wyndham House Poultry

Every effort has been made to verify that the information in this directory is correct. Please inform the publisher of any errors or omissions.
For the most current information please visit: www.civicbooks.com or www.boroughmarket.org.uk.